THE ROYAL HORTICULTURAL SOCIETY
PRACTICAL

PAT
AVING

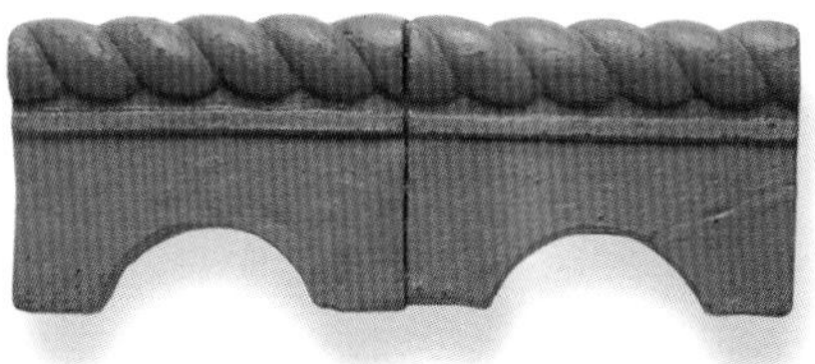

THE ROYAL HORTICULTURAL SOCIETY
PRACTICAL GUIDES

PATHS AND PAVING

DK
DORLING KINDERSLEY
LONDON • NEW YORK • SYDNEY • MOSCOW
www.dk.com

LONDON, NEW YORK, MUNICH,
MELBOURNE, DELHI

SERIES EDITOR Pamela Brown
SERIES ART EDITOR Stephen Josland
DESIGNER Alison Donovan

MANAGING EDITOR Louise Abbott
MANAGING ART EDITOR Lee Griffiths

DTP DESIGNER Matthew Greenfield

PRODUCTION Ruth Charlton, Mandy Inness

First published in Great Britain in 1999
Reprinted 2002
by Dorling Kindersley Limited,
80 Strand, London WC2R 0RL

A Penguin Company

A CIP catalogue for this book is available from the British Library.
ISBN 0 7513 47175

Reproduced by Colourscan, Singapore
Printed and bound by Star Standard Industries, Singapore

See our complete catalogue at
www.dk.com

  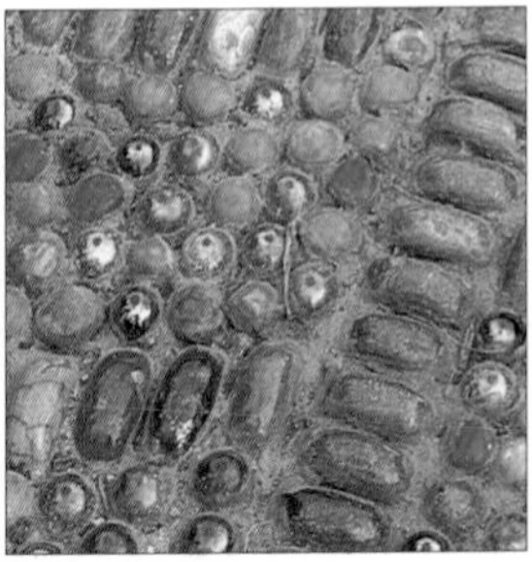

CONTENTS

PATHS AND PAVING IN THE GARDEN

WHY USE HARD SURFACES?

EVERY GARDENER KNOWS THE VALUE of soil and also understands that the best place for it is in the border, not on shoes. The practical advantages of hard surfaces are the first reason why paths criss-cross our gardens – but then we realize that, with the huge range of materials and effects available, they can enhance our garden designs and plantings and be beautiful in their own right.

EASY ACCESS

Hard surfaces make it easy to get around the garden, whether it is simply from the front gate to the house door or through the borders and down to the compost heap. At the most basic level, they provide clean, all-weather access to any part of the garden. If carefully chosen, they also look decorative and can be planned to blend with and enhance the materials, colour and style of surrounding buildings or nearby planting; a riven stone or gravel path, for example, would suit a rock garden. For those for whom gardening is a chore, not a passion, hard surfaces are a labour-saving way to cover ground. They do not preclude colour from plants because these can be grown in tubs, pots and raised beds.

► DEFINING A ROUTE
Using attractive and sympathetic materials to provide a little variation on the quickest route from A to B makes this path a strong design element, linking the house and garden in a most satisfying way.

PERFECT PAVING
A paved area provides all-weather access and a neutral, light-reflective base colour that is a perfect foil for this low-maintenance planting.

Architectural Framework

Whatever the style of your garden, hard materials make up a structural framework for its design. They provide an architectural "skeleton" that underlies, frames and enhances softer elements provided by plantings. And while all hard materials need to be functional and durable, you should bear in mind that they represent the single most important element in linking house and garden. As such, hard surfaces will provide the most aesthetic pleasure if you choose materials that blend, match or tone with the materials used in the house.

Changing Levels

The use of hard landscaping to create different levels introduces an added element of interest and allows features or focal points to be seen from more than one angle. A sloping garden can be laid out as a succession of gentle gradients, with either sweeping paths or terraces. Terrace beds can be retained with low walls or timber, using slopes or steps to link them. Wide steps can be used to display pots, while narrow, meandering steps between tall plantings create an air of mystery – the lure of something hidden just around the corner.

STEPS AND PAVING
Where space does not permit a gentle gradient, a series of steps securely built from hard landscaping materials is essential to make changes in level safely negotiable. If carefully planned, steps can also provide an irresistible lure to explore hidden features or, conversely, may offer the potential for a series of views from different heights over the remainder of the garden.

◀ ADAPTABLE GRAVEL
Loose materials like gravel are practical, economical and stylish, blending well with a wide range of other materials, such as cobbles and decking.

▼ FORMAL PATTERN
Even flat and level areas can be given definition and interest by laying simple paving materials (here brick) *in imaginative ways and introducing slight changes of level.*

Places to Pause

Narrow, straight paths are often purely functional routes to get from one point to another, but when they open out into a broader area, the natural reaction is to pause and look at the surroundings. Here is an opportunity to be adventurous and to combine different types of surface. A rough-textured surface, for example, can be used naturally to slow the pace and signal an opportunity to enjoy a vista that has opened up before you. A variation in colour or texture can also be exploited as a visual marker. Use it to proclaim a change in level or direction, or to define a separation between different areas of the garden, thus creating the boundaries of a succession of garden "rooms".

Use colour or texture to define different areas of the garden

Easy Maintenance

In comparison with a grass path, most hard surfaces represent considerable investment in time and money, but the long-term advantage is that once laid, most require minimal effort to keep them neat. Usually all that is needed is an occasional sweep or a scrub to remove algal growth that may have accumulated in damp weather. Wooden decking needs regular applications of stain or preservative to extend its life and to keep it looking pristine.

SITING A PAVED AREA

THE SITING OF A PAVED AREA depends largely on its proposed purpose, and its function will also dictate the most suitable materials. It makes sense, for example, to site a patio for dining and entertaining within easy reach of the kitchen door, or to place an area for repose and quiet relaxation in a secluded place away from hustle and bustle. And the materials used should be chosen to withstand the expected amount of traffic, or wear and tear.

SIZE AND SHAPE

While the shape of a paved area is largely a matter of taste, it is important to consider whether the shape you desire can easily be constructed in the material of your choice without complicated cutting to fit. An area whose outline is composed of straight edges or long, sweeping curves is not only the easiest to construct, it is also the most likely to confer an elegant simplicity on the overall design of your garden.

But perhaps the most important factor to consider is the dimensions. It is easy to make such areas too small, partly because the human eye perceives scale differently indoors and out. Paved areas need to be large enough to allow for comfortable, unrestricted movement, whatever activities you propose for the site. For example, a minimum width of two metres is essential to permit comfortable seating around a dining table. This must obviously be larger if you also wish to incorporate other features such as a barbecue. And if you wish to decorate areas with pots, planters or other garden furniture, surfaces need to be clear of clutter that may cause accidents.

PATIO FOR OUTDOOR LIVING
It makes sense to site a patio for dining within easy reach of the back door. Here, honey-toned paving brightens without reflective glare.

A SECLUDED NICHE
In shade, lead the way to secluded areas with a path that can easily be kept clear of slippery mud, mosses and algae.

Siting in Sun or Shade

In summer, a shady sitting area is a cooling refuge from the heat of the day, particularly if surrounded by lush foliage. But in deep shade, damp surfaces are prone to algal and moss growth, especially in winter and spring, so the material used must be easy to clean. Rough-textured materials will become attractively mossy without danger of accidents, but glossy surfaces, such as tiles, should be avoided. Dark-stained wood is sympathetic in shade but needs regular treatment with a wood preservative to eliminate slippery mosses.

> Dark-stained wood is visually sympathetic in shady areas

Most common materials are suitable for sunny areas. Stone and paving reflect heat and can make a sun trap in summer, yet remain pleasant and accessible in winter. Surface texture is seen most clearly in sun and any patternwork will be greatly enhanced. Bear in mind that light-coloured materials reflect glare uncomfortably in bright sun; soft tones of honey-gold or dove-grey lighten without such harsh reflectivity.

SECURITY ASPECTS

Pots, ornaments and garden furniture left out overnight can be a security worry, but you can take steps to reduce the risks:

- Secure pots, tubs and garden benches with bolts set in concrete or between slabs.
- Grow plants in sunken pots between the paving, or in large heavy tubs that are not easily lifted.
- Use gravel or stone chippings to provide a noisy deterrent underfoot.
- Install garden lighting for security and to enhance the area at night.
- Avoid screening with tall plants that can provide cover for intruders.

Routing the Path

PATHS ARE ROUTES FOR TRAVEL and there is little point linking two places where no one wants to walk. Before starting, identify the most travelled routes in the garden and use these as a basis for the plan. Then look at aesthetic considerations and adapt routes to accommodate the shapes of lawns and borders and to give views through the garden. A formal plan will require straight tracks that bisect the area while an informal design can have intricately twisting paths.

Getting from A to B

When planning paths for practical, all-weather garden access, it is important to choose a surface that is easy to walk on. This may be something as simple as concrete, which can be given an interesting finish (*see pp.44–45*) to prevent grey "runways" crossing the garden. If gravel is your preferred choice, use a grade that is large enough not to wedge in the soles of your shoes but small enough to allow you to walk on it comfortably (*see p.49*).

Where paths will be used frequently – especially by children – try to plan along "desire lines". Desire lines usually run along the shortest distance between two points; if the path is on an inconvenient route, it will not be taken. Curved corners

DIRECTLY TO YOUR DOOR
In some situations, the most appropriate route between A and B is a straight line. This short, front garden path is wide and straight enough to permit easy passage, especially when burdened with shopping, pushchairs or other domestic paraphernalia. This harmonious layout illustrates how even the strictly functional can be made attractive. Its style and colours match both the period of the house and the materials used in its construction.

▲ ACCESS TO A BORDER
A series of stepping stones provides practical access across a border. It allows plants to be tended and protects hidden bulbs or dormant plants from inadvertent treading.

◄ A MEANDERING PATH
The sinuous curves of this path invite exploration by suggesting that there are hidden features just around the next corner.

on a path will prevent shortcuts being taken across right-angled bends, which usually result in worn lawns or trodden borders. And curves are infinitely easier to negotiate with a wheelbarrow or mower.

Paths do not always need to be paved or gravelled. Small paths of stepping stones provide useful access through borders to tend the plants. Grass paths at the back of deep borders are handy for occasional access when a hedge needs trimming.

Leading the Eye

One of the main design functions to consider when laying a path is how it will draw the eye from one area to another. A straight path tends to reveal all, but if a focal feature concludes the vista, it pleases the eye. This need not mean that all of the garden is seen at once – site other paths so that they are discovered only as the main path is traversed. For most people, a curved path, which seldom reveals the garden in one sweep, is too tempting to leave unexplored. A seat at the crossroads of paths will allow enjoyment of several views from a single point, but it can lack a sense of privacy. A resting place in a niche at the end of a path makes a secluded spot from which to contemplate the plants as well as enjoy a view.

For most people, a curved path is just too tempting to leave unexplored

More Practical Considerations

It is vitally important to consider the width of your proposed paths since it is all too easy to make them too narrow. Where surrounding planting is tall or overhanging, even an otherwise roomy path seems narrow and, in wet weather, will be impossible to traverse without getting a soaking as you brush past. Low, creeping plants – even when they are used to soften hard edges – can also encroach on the width, and usefulness, of an access path.

Suiting Style and Purpose

Twists and turns in paths and steps lend character to a garden but are no fun if you are barrowing compost along them. Take time choosing routes and identifying their primary purpose. The formal style of a parterre, for example, positively demands narrow paths set at right angles to each other to enclose small beds, but this style of garden seldom calls for heavy barrow work. If access for garden equipment is needed regularly, wide paths with rounded corners will be more appropriate. Curves should be broad and sweeping rather than tight and wiggling – generous curves are easier to negotiate as well as to construct. If changes in level are to be negotiated using steps, consider the height of risers and width of tread. Broad shallow steps allow easy passage with barrow or mower; deeper steps are suited only to foot traffic.

▲ADDING LIGHT
Adequate and attractive lighting not only renders these steps safe in the dark, it brings an added dimension to the design at night.

▼FOCAL POINT
Generous paths add to the impact of a garden feature, while small pavers make a safe surface and are easily laid in a circular design.

SUNKEN GARDEN
This sunken garden is an attractive feature, but is less than ideal for a family garden used by small children or infirm adults. The change in level would be safer to negotiate had a shallow-stepped entrance been incorporated into the feature. Lighting would improve safety at night.

SAFE AND EASY ACCESS

The surfaces of main paths must be kept clear of clutter if they are not to prove a potential cause of accidents. Take this into account and make them sufficiently wide if they are to be lined with plants, pots or other ornaments, thus combining use with beauty. Ample width is especially important where paths meet to form a crossroads, particularly if you wish to use the opportunity to create a focal point shared by all the paths.

Keep paths that are in frequent use free of hazardous clutter

Where paths take unexpected turns, or if steps must be used regularly in the dark, it is worth installing lighting; lights confer safety and security and also bring life and atmosphere to the garden at night.

The surface of paths and steps is also a vital safety consideration. While textural variation often plays an important role in a design, it is best restricted to margins or other areas of light traffic. Level, even and non-slip surfaces are essential for safe access, especially if they are to be used by the very young, very old or infirm.

PLANNING PATHS

- Make paths wide enough to allow easy access; allow 1.5m for free access along practical paths for barrowing or for two people to walk side by side.
- Keep path networks simple.
- Make sure paving surfaces are non-slip, level and even. Keep textural changes level with adjacent surfaces. Restrict any raised textural detail to areas of low traffic.
- Make changes in level obvious to avoid the chance of tripping.
- Make steps of equal (therefore predictable) depth and width; they should not be too steep. Highlight edges with a paler material and use lighting at night time for extra safety.

DECORATIVE SURFACES

PAVING SERVES MORE THAN A PRACTICAL PURPOSE – if materials are carefully chosen, it can be beautiful to look at, can link house and garden and provide a perfect foil for plantings. But with such a wealth of materials available, there is always a temptation to use too many, resulting in a busy and distracting effect. The most pleasing results will be gained with a restricted range of materials, selected to tie in with the style and colour of the house and other garden features.

UNITY AND VARIETY

The overriding principle designers use when choosing decorative materials is to strike a balance between unity and variety. Although it is easy to unite a single material with the other materials used in a garden, a large expanse is likely to look monotonous and will need a little variety to bring it to life.

Large areas of slabs can be broken up by interspersing them, for example, with lines of bricks or terracotta tiles laid on edge. Gravel and stones laid in concrete can also break up stark areas of paving. You can use contrasts in colour or texture to mark out main routes or delineate areas for seating or dining. Changes of level can be incorporated into a paving plan and will add visual appeal, especially in the form of steps or raised beds.

In large expanses of paving, you can make spaces for planting by leaving out occasional slabs or, alternatively, avoid monotony by placing attractive pots and tubs of plants on the paved surface.

MIXING MATERIALS
Wooden decking with colour-matched gravel (above) *ties in a path with a wooden raised bed. A large area of paving* (right) *is relieved by an elegant contrast of colour and texture created by setting in a panel of water-worn pebbles.*

STYLIZED PAVING
Here, a simple gravel surface tones perfectly with the dominant feature while subtle colour and textural contrast is provided by stepping stones. The stone lantern has inspired a thoughtful selection of a limited range of materials which have then been used to create an appropriate oriental-style setting.

Using Texture and Colour

When choosing colours and textures, take note of – and try to blend with – those used in the house and other features. In country gardens, you may also wish to consider the surrounding landscape. The synthetic tints of brightly coloured paving look unnatural in rural areas and seldom blend well with materials used in older properties. Here, recycled materials with an aged appearance may look best. But in modern urban gardens, bright colours combine well with painted walls, stylish ceramics or furniture. In general, though, more subtle textural contrasts, using the natural palette of warm browns, cool greys and terracotta, are easiest to place.

> Brightly coloured materials can work well in urban gardens

Timber is particularly versatile: it can be stained in natural or bright colours and, in itself, provides a variety of textures, from rough-hewn to smooth and planed. Use colour and textural contrasts to define path or patio edges, to enliven large areas of paving, or simply to add interest to areas designated for seating.

CHOOSING MATERIALS

In most cases, good results are achieved by using materials that already exist in the garden. The colour and fabric of the house will probably be the main influence on your choice of paving material. For a brick-built house, for example, paving edged with or made from brick or terracotta tiles would suit. Similarly, aged brick and mellow timber complement the honey tones of sandstone.

If the garden is to include wooden features such as a summerhouse or pergola, timber decking may be an appropriate choice.

A rock garden may dictate the colour of a nearby stone path – materials from the same local source will usually blend perfectly.

Mimicking Nature

Creators of gardens have long sought inspiration from the natural world and, for many gardeners, natural effects are still the most prized. A path that mimics a dried-up river bed, studded with colonizing plants, is not only a route through the garden, but an opportunity to grow a greater diversity of plants. Crushed slate or gravel resembles a mountain scree and makes an ideal home for alpine plants, while sea-washed pebbles make a perfect foil for maritime plants, such as sea lavender or thrift. In coastal gardens, crushed shells make a good, crunchy path if laid like gravel.

> Display maritime plants next to a path of sea-washed pebbles

Timber is a natural choice for a woodland setting and slabs of tree trunk, set among bark chippings, look perfectly appropriate. Railway sleepers are ideal for constructing long-lasting paths and are very effective if set in bark or gravel and interplanted with species native to the woodland floor.

Abstract Design

Small modern plots lend themselves well to experiments with abstract designs and, here you might seek inspiration from the works of modern artists. A geometric, hard-edged layout of different materials can form a

▲ RECLAIMED MATERIALS
Old railway sleepers, which are impregnated with bitumen, make a long-lasting material for imaginative paths. As with other reclaimed materials, they come ready-aged and mellow.

► A RIVER OF SLATE
Japanese and Chinese garden makers take inspiration from, and echo, the natural world. Here, a ribbon of crushed slate suggests a babbling brook in contrast to the limpid water contained within the tsukubai, *a traditional ornamental bowl.*

framework for plants to create a living patchwork of colour. Here, caution can be thrown to the wind; mundane paving can be set beside materials of bright colour with the spaces between filled with plants and gravel. Areas of the patchwork can be made into smaller individual compositions, with planting that coordinates with the paving materials. A chequered pattern of slabs and soil is a popular way to grow

> Throw caution to the wind and offset mundane paving with bright colour

herbs, alpines and bulbs, allowing the plants to grow through gravel or chippings. Parcelling up an area into smaller units often means that you can eke out relatively costly materials over a fairly large area without breaking the bank. In small areas, you can be as creative as you like: expensive materials such as glass beads or polished pebbles can be placed alongside contrasting evergreen plants, or broken ceramic tiles used to create picture mosaics

CHEQUERED COURSE
An abstract design parcelled into small units can eke out expensive decorative materials to cover a relatively large area.

or elaborate designs. And do not underestimate the value of reclaimed, recycled or found objects, for their use can often put a highly individual mark on your designs. Timber, whether new or reclaimed, can be painted or stained to add an extra dimension and interesting textures in the garden.

INSPIRATION

- Visit friends' gardens and those open to the public armed with a notebook. Jot down any exciting uses of materials that catch your eye. Modify them to make them your own.
- Builders' yards and recycling centres may get you buzzing with ideas; don't overlook the plumbers' merchants – utilitarian copper items acquire an attractive verdigris with age.
- Magazines and books on gardening are rich sources of visual stimulation, but so too are those concerned with interior design.
- Look to nature; the seashore, the forest floor, mountain screes and water margins all hold inspiration for the observant gardener.

Finishing Touches

THE EDGING AND PLANTS AROUND a path can greatly enhance its appearance. Edging prevents loose material from spreading into flower beds; low, creeping plants disguise harsh edges and bring a natural look to new paths. If plants that overhang main paths are kept to no higher than shoulder height, it helps to increase the impression of width. To accentuate a formal look, choose a low plant, such as lavender or bergenia, and grow it along both sides or at regular intervals.

Adding Plants

In sunny parts of the garden, fragrant plants such as herbs, silver-leaved pinks and lavender are a good choice for path edges, and will release their fragrance as you brush past them. Creeping plants such as thymes and camomile can be put into gaps between slabs or grown through gravel, but avoid putting clumps in the way of the main access paths where they may not survive treading and might cause an accident. They are ideal beneath seats where they can be enjoyed at leisure and their fragrance will heighten your sense of relaxation. Put pots and containers of temporary and permanent plants at the

COOL CONTRAST
The colour warmth of the hard materials used in this design draws the eye and lifts the beauty of this cool-colour border to higher levels. Scented plants release fragrance as they are brushed against providing another, more ethereal dimension. The height gained by the judicious siting of a planted terracotta urn – blending seamlessly with warm brick paving – reflects and echoes the rising steps that terminate the vista.

edges of paving to help the hard surface blend into the surrounding planting, or in groups to break up the effect of large areas.

Soft Edging

Neat plants make a good edging for paths. Among the most popular is dwarf box, which can be clipped to keep it to just 15cm. Lavender and santolina can also be clipped as a formal low hedge. A formal look can be enhanced by the symmetrical planting of architectural plants, such as yuccas, at intervals along the length of a path. London pride (*Saxifraga* × *urbium*), bergenias and pinks make low cushions of foliage and are evergreen. Hostas are excellent edging plants and, with their wide variation in leaf size, can match, or contrast with, the surface. Brick paving accentuates the size of large-leaved varieties; smaller-leaved hostas are in scale with narrow paths. Although hostas are deciduous, they can be underplanted with spring-flowering bulbs. When these start to die down, the hostas will disguise their yellowing foliage.

Hostas are excellent edging plants, with a wide variety of leaf sizes

▲ INFORMAL EDGING
Neat, rosette-forming alpines, like this semperviνum, quickly colonize gritty planting pockets between paving.

▼ FORMAL EDGING
The precise line of these period edging tiles accentuates the neat, crisp finish of this immaculately clipped dwarf box hedge.

PLANTS FOR PAVED AREAS

FOR PLANTING POCKETS
Acaena microphylla
Ajuga reptans
Alchemilla (most)
Armeria maritima
Aubrieta (many)
Ceratostigma
Erinus alpinus
Euphorbia cyparissias
E. myrsinites
Festuca glauca
Hebe (many)
Helianthemum (many)
Jovibarba (many)
Lamium maculatum
Ophiopogon planiscapus
Persicaria affinis
Phlox subulata
Plantago nivalis
Potentilla alba
Pratia (most)
Raoulia australis
Rhodanthemum
Salvia officinalis
Saponaria ocymoides
Saxifraga × *urbium*
Sedum (many)
Sempervivum (most)
Sisyrinchium striatum
Stachys byzantina
Viola riviniana Purpurea Group
Yucca filamentosa

FOR FRAGRANCE
Artemisia caucasica
A. schmidtiana
A. stelleriana
Chamaemelum nobile 'Treneague'*
Mentha pulegium
*M. requienii**
Salvia officinalis
*Thymus serpyllum**

* withstands treading

HARD EDGING

A neat, permanent edging is the perfect way to finish a path. It is aesthetically pleasing and, by retaining border soil and preventing the path becoming muddied, it is also practical. Modern reproductions of traditional Victorian terracotta rope tiles, while expensive, are durable and suit both formal and informal schemes.

Reclaimed materials can be both practical and inexpensive

Concrete kerbing is cheap and appropriate in modern settings, but for more elegant effects, there are prettier alternatives such as cast stone edging. Reclaimed materials like roof tiles and timber are both practical and inexpensive, and, with imagination, can make unusual edges to paths.

PATIO DECORATION

A diverse range of pots, tubs and urns is available to provide decoration for patios. Filled with tender plants, they can lend the illusion of tropical warmth during the summer months, while spring bedding provides colour early in the year. A garden

LAWN MEETS PAVING
A hard edge is softened as turf penetrates the cracks between the pavers. Make sure pavers are lower than the turf for easy mowing.

ornament set amongst them, or isolated to emphasize its presence, will complete the effect. But whether you use a group of pots or ornaments, or a single large one as a focal point, for safety's sake, do not place them on busy corners and keep them to the edges on steps and main routes. If used with discretion and grouped with regard to their size and height, they elevate a design without creating clutter.

FORMAL EDGING
Modern, moulded clay edging tiles are frost-resistant and make a neat and durable edge for formal borders.

SEASHELL EDGING
Seashells add a pretty and whimsical feel to edging, but avoid those with a sharp edge in gardens where children have access.

LAYING PATHS AND SURFACES

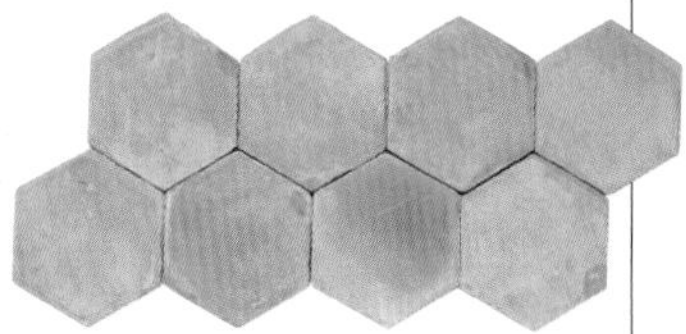

RIGID PAVING

THE FOLLOWING PAGES cover a selection of simple projects using a range of materials and techniques that gardeners with few building skills – or none at all – can tackle safely and confidently to produce satisfying results in usually no more than a weekend. Bear in mind that the durability of all surfaces depends on the use of construction methods appropriate to each type of material, and that the true cost includes not only initial outlay, but also the degree of maintenance required and the expected lifespan. Rigid paving (*see p.25*) made from preformed slabs – available in a wealth of shapes, sizes and colours – is one of the most expensive, but provided that slabs are securely laid onto a properly prepared base, they last for many decades. Flexible paving (*see p.35*), made from cobbles, setts or bricks bedded on sand, is also expensive, but hard-wearing. It may lift or sag in places with age, and need a little attention. Gravel (*see p.49*), although one of the most attractive and least costly of materials, may need replenishing regularly and demands frequent attention to weed control. Although relatively cheap, durable and easy to lay, concrete (*see p.41*) has a utilitarian image that belies its versatility in the creation of decorative surfaces. Wooden decking (*see p.57*) is extremely stylish and moderately expensive. It is simple to construct and, if treated with suitable preservatives, has an expected life of 25 years or more.

FLEXIBLE PAVING

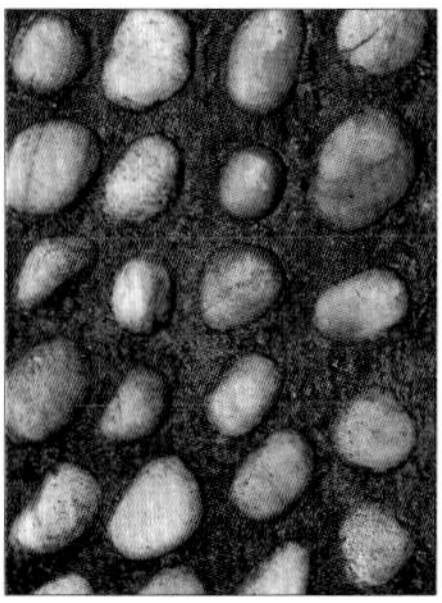

DECORATIVE CONCRETE

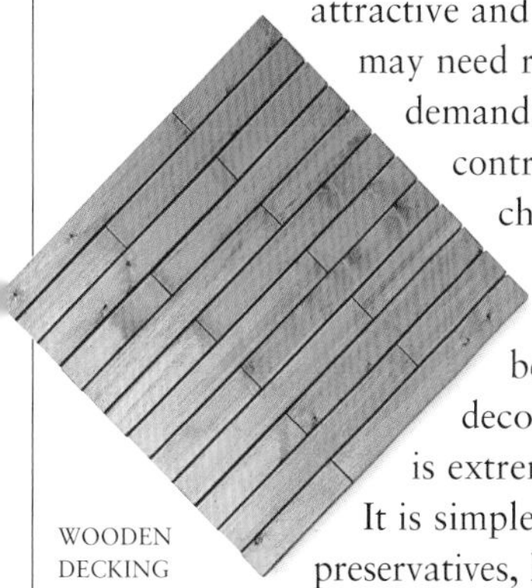

WOODEN DECKING

FORMAL PAVING

TO MAKE FORMAL, smooth, permanent paving bedded onto and jointed with mortar, and add clearly defined, well-built steps and low walls, you need to use professional construction methods and to pay strict attention to levels and measurements, because an unsatisfactory result will be hard to remedy. A firm foundation is crucial, because if it moves, slabs may crack. Provided that the project is not too ambitious, the building skills involved are not hard to master.

LAYING PERMANENT PAVING

The laying of any permanent surface should be carefully thought through before you even visit the builders' merchant. Deciding the location, shape and materials to be used and how best to lay them depends on factors such as how much use or traffic the surface will receive, the relative size of the garden, and the materials used in existing buildings and structures.

The essence of formal style lies in balanced symmetry and crisp geometry which is, in practical terms, most easily achieved by laying slabs of uniform size and shape, as here, on firm foundations. You can relax the style to include softer lines and curves by using variably sized materials such as crazy paving, small, warm-toned units such as bricks laid in patterns and spirals, or pavers that are specially shaped to produce circular designs.

BEFORE YOU START

- Before undertaking any excavation work, locate underground utilities, such as water or gas pipes and electricity, television or telephone cables, to avoid damaging them. You must leave inspection covers unobstructed.
- Any surface that butts up directly to a house wall must finish at least 15cm below any damp-proof course and incorporate a slight drainage slope (*see overleaf*) that sheds water away from the house foundations.
- You should not walk on the paving, once laid, for 24 hours, or ideally two days – do not pave yourself into a corner. Think about how you will keep traffic off the area.

FOUNDATION FOR PAVING *The key to success with paving is in the preparation of a firm and level base, built up from several layers of materials.*

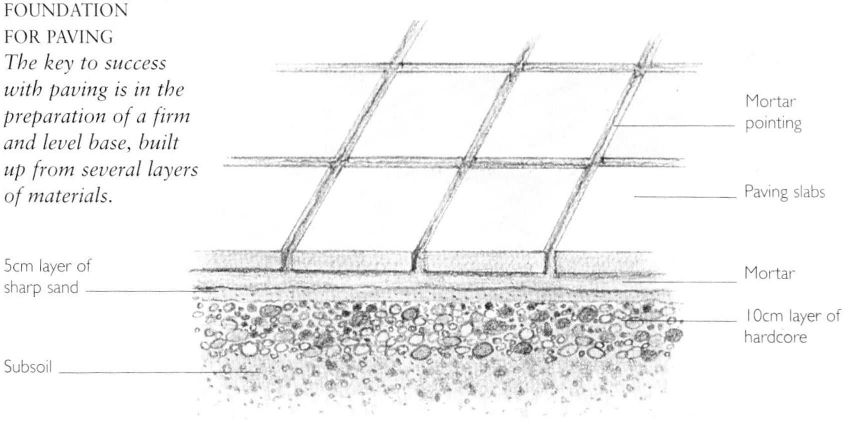

◄ OFFSET SLABS *Cutting some slabs allows unobtrusive patterning instead of a rigid chequerboard.*

YOU NEED:

MATERIALS
- Hardcore to cover area to compacted depth of 10cm
- Sharp sand to cover hardcore to depth of 5cm
- Slabs (allow an extra 5% of total quantity for breakages if you need to cut to size)
- Ready-mixed mortar mix
- Edging of choice (*see p.28*)

TOOLS
- Marking pegs
- String • Builder's square • Spade
- Spirit level
- Bolster chisel
- Club hammer
- Timber plank
- Builder's trowel
- Spacers (1cm dowel cut into 5cm lengths)
- Jigger (optional)
- Brush

TOOL HIRE
- Plate compacter

LAYING THE FOUNDATIONS

1 **Use pegs and string** to mark out the area to be paved. Check that the corners are at right angles using a builder's square.

2 **Dig down** to firm subsoil; allow 15cm for hardcore and sand plus the depth of the surface layer. Tamp with plate compacter.

3 **Insert marking pegs** in a grid at 2m intervals as level guides. Incorporate a slight fall (*see* drainage slope, *below*) to allow surface water to drain away. Use a spirit level to ensure pegs and string are level.

4 **Add a layer** of hardcore; compact to 10cm and check levels. Add an 8cm layer of sand and compact to 5cm.

DRAINAGE SLOPE

A surface should slope with a fall of about 2.5cm per 2m to permit surface drainage. If it abutts the house, it must be 15cm below the damp-proof course. Mark a number of pegs, at the same distance from the top end of each. Knock them in, in rows 2m apart – the first row at the top of the slope with the marks at soil level. In the second row, put a 2.5cm offcut on each peg. Lay a spirit level on a plank between this peg and one in the first row. Adjust the height of the lower peg so the top of the offcut and the upper peg are level. Remove the offcut. Repeat down the slope.

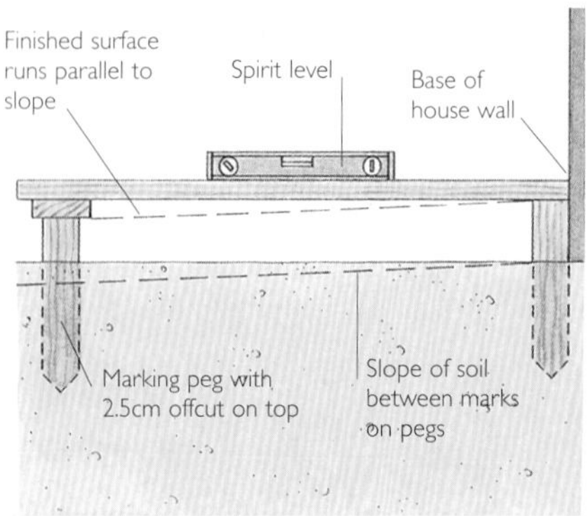

CUTTING PAVING SLABS TO FIT

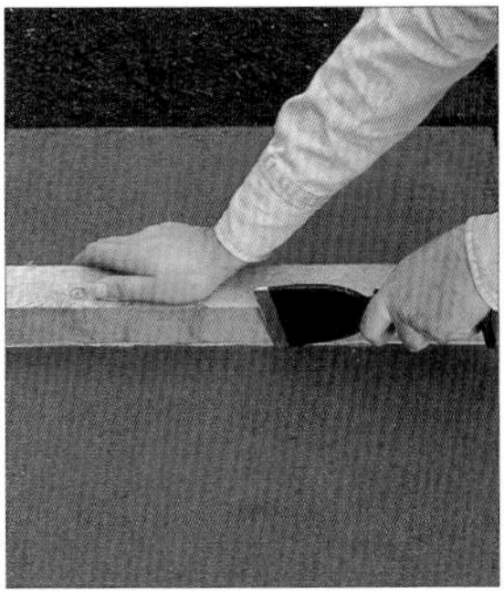

1 **On a flat,** firm surface, use a bolster chisel blade to score a groove on both faces and edges of the slab.

2 **Work along** the scored line with a bolster chisel and club hammer to deepen the groove on the slab.

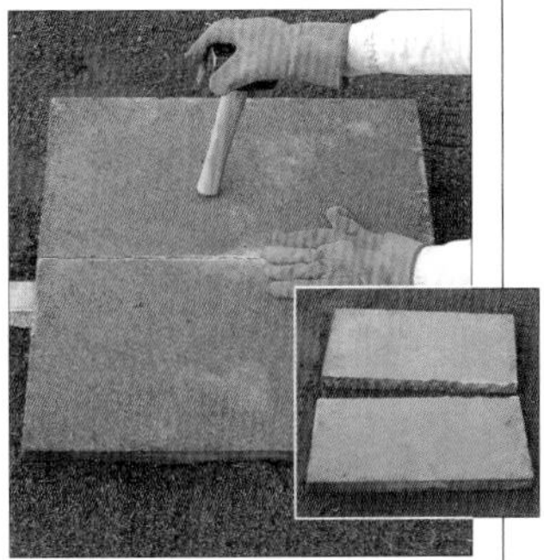

3 **Place the slab** on a length of timber. Align the groove with timber edge; tap the slab with hammer until it splits.

LAYING THE PAVING SLABS

1 **Start laying the slabs** at the house wall or other defined edge. Spread strips of mortar in a square just smaller than the slab. Add a cross strip for large slabs.

2 **Position the slab** on the mortar and tap it down. Use a spirit level to check that it is level. Repeat over the area, using spacers to create 1cm mortar gaps between the slabs.

3 **Take out the spacers** before the mortar sets. After 2 days or so, fill in between the slabs with stiff mortar. An easy way of doing this is to use a jigger (*inset*). Aligning the central slit of this device and the gap between 2 slabs allows the gap to be filled without spilling mortar on the slabs. Tamp down the mortar so it is recessed by 2mm. Brush the slabs clean.

Finishing off Patios and Paving

Once the slabs have been laid, the surface may be finished with edging. Edging serves a number of purposes, some practical, others decorative. Most immediately, it defines an area, separating it from adjacent lawns and flower beds. On a more practical level, when a surface is made up using flexible material, edging holds that material in place and confines it within the desired area. You can use the same material for edging, or introduce another surface to contrast with and complement the principal paving. In terms of style, the more decorative the edging, the less formal the finish. Possible materials include wood, brick, pavers and tiles. If using wood, make sure that it has been pressure-treated with preservative. Bricks, tiles or pavers should be mortared in so there is no chance of them shifting on the base.

PAVERS AS EDGING
Pavers create a neat finish to a patio's edge. The diagram (right) *shows how simple they are to put in place. Set below the level of the adjacent lawn, they permit easy mowing.*

PAVERS AS EDGING

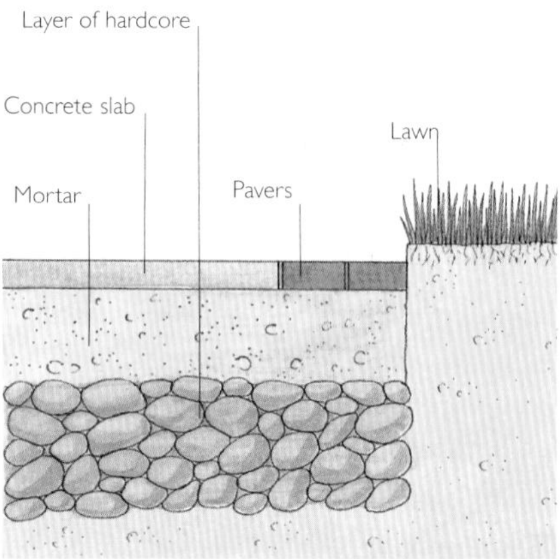

MIXED MATERIAL EDGING
Here, a mixture of treated wooden stumps and pavers are set in concrete to produce an attractive edge to a patio. A raised edge keeps plants and loose mulches within bounds.

MIXED MATERIAL EDGING

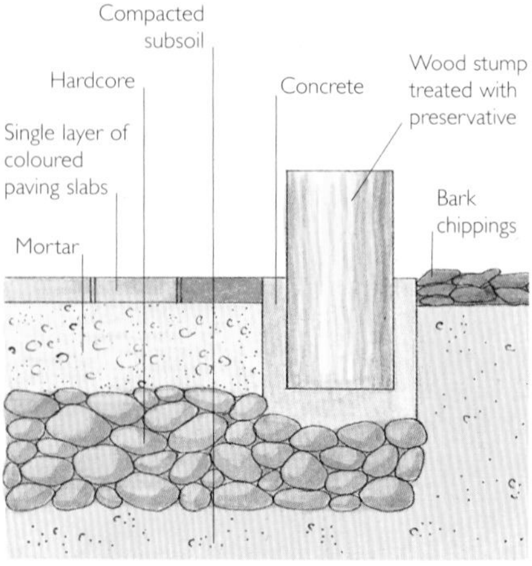

Alternative Formal Surfaces

A range of materials such as bricks, setts and crazy paving, whether found, reclaimed or purchased, can be used for formal surfaces. They must be capable of providing an even, non-slip surface for walking and sufficiently robust to withstand severe weather conditions. Their strength should match the load that they have to bear – whether it is foot or vehicular traffic, for example.

BRICK PAVING
Bricks make an even and attractive hard surface. If using reclaimed bricks, make sure that they are weatherproof; stock bricks, used for facing houses, for example, tend to flake if subjected to a freeze-thaw cycle.

Preformed Paving Slabs

Garden centres stock a variety of preformed paving slabs which can be fitted together to form a complete surface. Flexible units in circular, octagonal and interlocking shapes come in a range of materials and colours. Some units look like several fitted together. They are quickly and easily laid to create complex and finely textured effects. "Keyed" blocks or slabs are specially designed for the construction of curves and circles without complex cutting.

KEYED SLABS

MOULDED CEMENT SLAB

BRICK-EFFECT SLAB

HEXAGONAL TERRACOTTA TILE BLOCK

Laying Crazy Paving

To make a really smooth, safe surface out of crazy paving, it is best to lay it on mortar, with bedding mortar filling the gaps for a more impervious surface. When laying the paving, position any edging material first, and secure it in place with mortar so that the boundaries are clearly defined or, as below, cut a straight edge in turf and butt the paving up against it. Working from one corner of the area, first loose-lay an area of about 1m square without mortar, fitting the pieces together like a jigsaw. Keep the gaps small. Once satisfied with their placement, lift and bed them on mortar. Check that they are level with the edge pieces, using a straight-edge and spirit level, before moving on to fill the rest of the area.

A UNIQUE FINISH
Here, sunshine dappled over crazy paving adds a lovely touch to the garden. The beauty of crazy paving is that each surface is unique.

1 **Using string lines** and pegs to mark the height of the edges, lay foundations (*see p.26*). Then lay the edging pieces, placing their straight edges outermost.

2 **Fill the centre** with large slabs, and infill with small ones. Using wood and a club hammer, bed them on blobs of mortar. Keep the central slabs level with edging pieces.

3 **Fill the cracks** with crumbly, almost dry mortar, or brush in sand. If using a dark-coloured stone such as slate, a concrete dye will make the cracks less conspicuous.

4 **If applying a mortar finish,** use a pointing trowel to bevel the mortar so that any surface water drains quickly away from the slabs.

Laying Bricks

For a house made of brick, using bricks to make a patio is a great way of visually linking it with the garden. Bricks are more versatile than stone or concrete slabs as they can be laid in a variety of patterns.

Such is the wide range of bricks available, it is easy to find a type that suits your surroundings. Contact local builders' merchants for large quantities and make sure that the bricks are frost-resistant.

1 **Prepare foundations** (*see p.26*), allowing space for edging bricks. For small areas, the sub-base can be tamped with a piece of wood rather than a plate compacter.

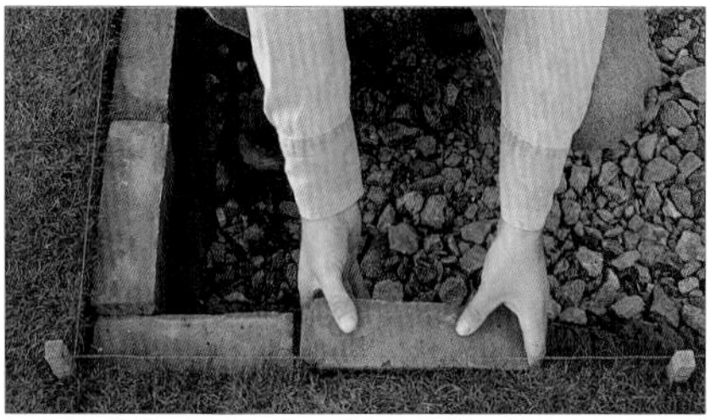

2 **Use string lines and pegs** to set edging bricks at desired height. If edges butt up to a lawn, make the finished level of edging just below the lawn surface for ease of mowing.

3 **Lay edging bricks** on a concrete footing and mortar the cracks. Bed the rest on blobs of bedding mortar; tamp them level. At intervals, check the levels in all directions.

4 **Spread a thin layer** of dry mortar over the surface of the brickwork and brush it between the cracks. Sprinkle with water (*inset*) to set the mortar; clean the surface.

LAYING BRICKS IN PATTERNS

Bricks may be laid in several simple ways to create attractive patterns, such as those shown here; the herringbone pattern requires bricks to be cut to fit at the margins of the area. Ideally, bricks should be laid on a 2.5cm layer of bedding mortar, but where edging bricks are fixed firmly in place and the sub-base is sound, they can be laid on sand (*see p.35*). Use thin strips of wood as spacers, if desired. Dry mortar used for pointing is self-setting in damp weather, but setting time can be speeded up by sprinkling with water as shown above.

WATTLEWEAVE

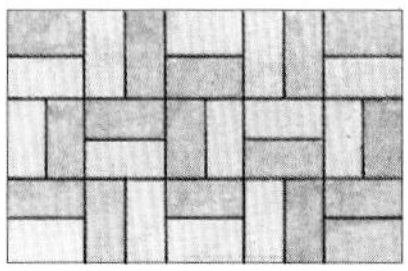

PARQUET/BASKETWEAVE

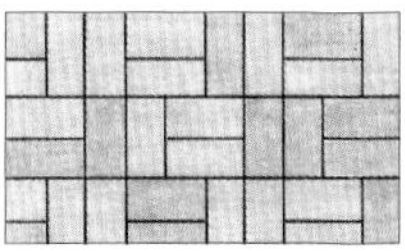

INTERLOCKING BOXES

HERRINGBONE

CHANGING LEVELS

There are a number of ways to change a flat, featureless garden into one that incorporates different levels. Low walls, steps and raised beds are all features that can eliminate the visual boredom of a single level. They add visual interest and can have practical benefits. A low wall, for example, can offer protection to bedding from wind and frost. Steps cut into a slope draw the eye into an area where previously there may only have been a bland grassy incline and make access across the garden much easier. Use the same, or toning, materials as the patio for a unifying effect (*see facing page*).

BUILDING A LOW WALL

A low wall, whether simply used to execute a change in level or to create a raised bed, is a simple DIY project. If less than a metre in height, it requires few technical skills and – although it is always wise to check – is unlikely to contravene local building regulations. When siting a low wall, consider whether it is to act as a barrier or whether you need to gain safe access across it. You may need to build in a step for any wall higher than 20–25cm, the maximum comfortable distance to step down safely without risk of jarring or stumbling.

A DEFINING WALL
This low wall of reconstituted stone blocks is quite easy to build and gives the raised lawn a neat and strongly defined boundary.

WALL FOUNDATIONS

A low wall must be built on a solid foundation such as a concrete block; this is bedded into the hardcore base of the adjacent paving so that the edge of the block aligns with the edge of the paving. Build the wall so that the first brick will be level with the paving, then insert a small-diameter pipe to form a drainage weephole (*right*), or leave one vertical crack between bricks on the next layer unfilled with mortar. Lay the paving so that the mortar extends over the edge of the concrete block to lock it in place and leave a 5cm gap between the paving and the wall. Fill this gap, and that between the wall and soil, with coarse gravel to stop the weephole from becoming clogged.

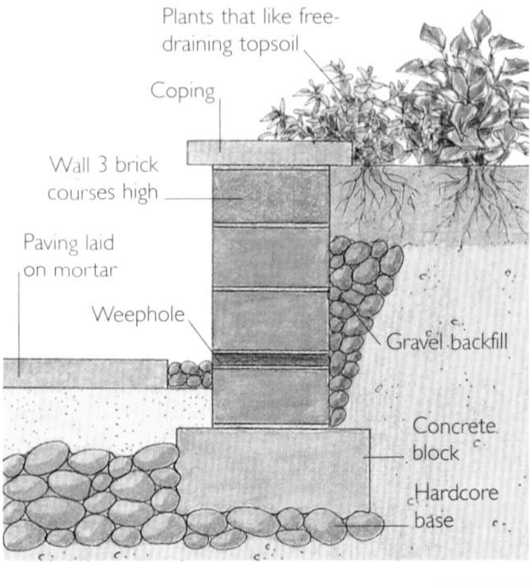

Constructing Simple Steps

Calculate the number of steps you need by dividing the height of the slope by the total height of one riser (including slab and mortar). To measure slope height, place a peg at the top of the slope and a post at the bottom. Tie string between the two so it is level with the top of the slope; measure the distance between the string and ground level.

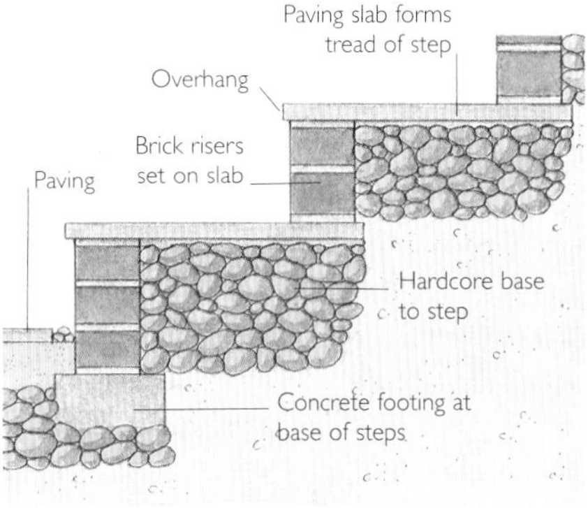

STEPPING SAFELY

Make treads at least 30cm deep from front to back, with a maximum 5cm overhang. The height of risers is normally 10–18cm.

Simple Steps with Paving Slabs

1 Use string and pegs to mark the sides of the steps, then run strings along the fronts of the treads. Dig out the steps and compact the earth for each tread area.

2 Make a footing 15cm deep and twice the brick width; fill with concrete over a 7cm hardcore base. Lay first riser on the set concrete footing; use string to check bricks are level.

3 Fill risers with hardcore to the height of the bricks and tamp down. Set the slabs on 1cm of mortar, with an overhang of 2.5–5cm at the front. Leave a small gap between them.

4 Mark the position of the second riser on the slabs; mortar the bricks in place. Fill in and set the treads as before. Continue with the remaining steps. Mortar between the slabs.

INFORMAL PAVING

WHEN YOU LAY OUT YOUR GARDEN in an informal style, you have free rein in the choice of materials for paving and other surfaces and for textural detail and colour combinations that would be out of place in formal gardens. However, the materials must still be practical and safe. Informal schemes lend themselves to flexible paving, bedded in sand and kept in place with a fixed edge. It is easy to lay and to replace single units and is more forgiving of mistakes.

MAKING AN INFORMAL PAVED AREA

A surface constructed from materials of varying shapes and sizes has integral textural variety that lends charm and interest of itself. Often, the most successful results are to be had by combining materials that share a common range of colour tone. Bear in mind the danger of creating busy and jumbled effects by using too many different elements of colour and texture.

FOR THE BEST RESULTS

- Ensure that walking surfaces are even and non-slip, keeping less regular, high-definition textures to the margins of an area.
- When using irregularly shaped units of different depths, adjust the depth at which each unit is bedded to create level surfaces.
- Use the aged, mellow appearance of reclaimed materials to introduce informality seamlessly into established gardens at relatively low cost.

ESSENTIAL CALCULATIONS
Do your maths first, especially if using found or reclaimed materials. Calculate roughly the size of each area to be filled with each different material so that you don't run out before the design is finished.

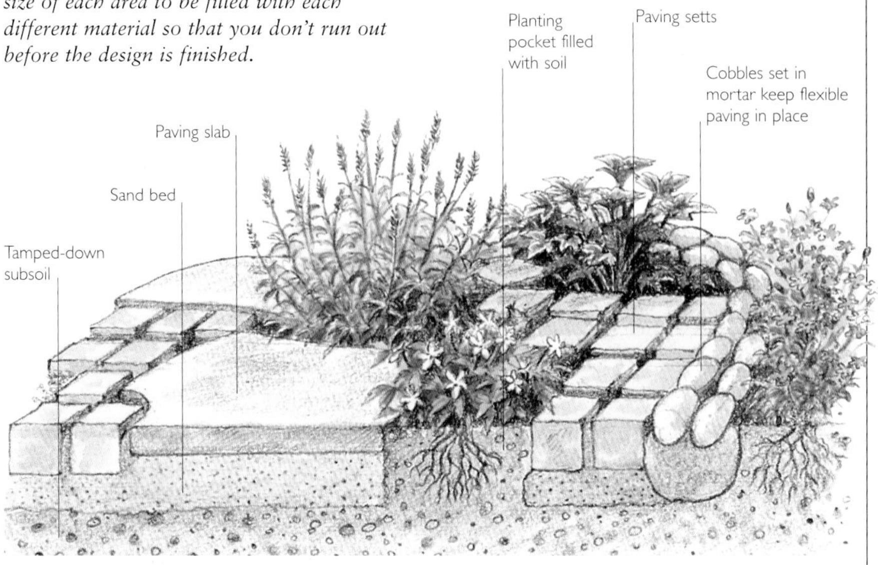

INFORMAL CURVES *A sinuous edging of cobbles borders loosely laid setts.*

YOU NEED:

MATERIALS

- Paving materials: paving slabs and granite setts
- Sharp sand for a 8cm covering of base area
- Cobbles to edge
- Ready-mixed mortar mix to bed cobbles

TOOLS

- Spade
- Wooden post
- Rake
- Trowel
- Spirit level
- Club hammer
- Brush • Bucket

PREPARING THE BASE

1 **Mark out** the area, then dig it out to form a level base of compacted soil (you can reserve the soil to use elsewhere). Make it deep enough to hold a 5cm layer of firmed sand plus the thickness of the slabs so that the paving will be level with its surrounds. Tamp small areas firm using a wooden post (*see p.31*). Use a plate compacter (*see p.67*) for larger areas.

2 **Add a layer** of sharp sand to cover the entire area; a depth of about 8cm will firm down to 5cm.

3 **Rake the sand** smooth, and level by eye, paying attention to filling any voids or irregularities at the edges.

4 **Firm the sand** to create a bedding layer. Tread down with your feet to give a final depth of about 5cm.

MAKING THE FIXED EDGE

1 **Arrange the edging cobbles** and, when satisfied, mortar in place. Settle them into the mortar a few at a time to form a level edge that is higher than surrounding beds.

2 **Place the largest pieces** of paving into position first on the sand bed. Add or subtract sand below each slab until they are all sitting level with each other.

3 **Check the level** of the slabs one with another using a spirit level. Tamp down with the handle of a club hammer. The slabs should also be level with surrounding beds.

4 **Lay the setts** approximately level with the slabs, adjusting height as necessary by scooping out more or less sand. Fit them fairly closely to prevent them moving.

5 **When the setts** are in place and settled securely into the sand, finish bedding them in by tamping them down firmly with the handle of a club hammer.

6 **Using a spirit level,** check that the setts are level with the slabs as you go. Leave some small areas unpaved to act as pockets for planting.

Finishing off the Paving

1 **Add a final layer** of dry sharp sand mixed with a little fine soil, using a trowel. Add enough sand and soil mix to cover the setts, slabs and any small gaps between them.

2 **Using a soft brush,** sweep the sand and soil mix into the gaps between setts and slabs. Remove any air pockets by firming the sand with a narrow piece of wood.

Planting Up the Pockets

1 To make a planting hole, first remove as much sand and soil mix as possible from the planting pocket. Scoop it into a bucket to keep the paving free of soil, then discard it.

2 Fill in the planting hole with a mixture of compost or topsoil and well-rotted organic matter. Use a trowel to work the mixture well into the surrounding soil.

3 Dig a hole for each plant, deep and wide enough to accommodate the root ball. Insert plant, backfill with compost mix; firm to eliminate any air pockets around the roots.

4 Sweep any spilled compost into the planting pocket before watering in the plant well. This avoids creating muddy patches. The area is then top-dressed (*see facing page*).

Planting in Crevices

To sow seed (right), *brush away grit top-dressing, if necessary; trickle in compost. Sow seed thinly, cover with a thin layer of grit and water in. Small plug plants establish rapidly. Make a planting hole with a dibber and insert the plant. Back-fill with compost. Firm and water in.*

SOWING SEED

USING PLUG PLANTS

TOP-DRESSING THE PLANTED AREA

When you have completed planting, top-dress all soil surfaces with a 1cm layer of grit or fine-grade gravel. This adds a unifying element to the design, and acts as a mulch, excluding light and helping to prevent the germination of weed seeds. Also, it will help to keep plant roots cool and moist in summer. A grit top-dressing around the necks of vulnerable plants, such as alpines and silver-leaved plants, provides excellent drainage and reduces the risk of fatal damage in cold, wet winters.

SUBSEQUENT MAINTENANCE
Keep the plants well watered while they are becoming established. Thereafter they need little additional water except during prolonged periods of dry weather. Keep the area free of weeds, by hand-weeding or by spot-weeding with a suitable weedkiller, following the manufacturer's instructions.

GOOD PLANTS FOR PAVING

PLANTS FOR POCKETS

Achillea clypeolata
Aethionema (most)
Alchemilla alpina, *A. conjuncta*
Anthemis punctata subsp. *cupaniana*
Arabis caucasica
Armeria maritima
Artemisia schmidtiana 'Nana'
Buxus microphylla 'Green Pillow'
Campanula arvatica, *C. carpatica*
Dianthus alpinus, *D. arenarius*
Euphorbia polychroma
Geranium clarkei, *G. dalmaticum*
Hebe cupressoides 'Boughton Dome'
Helichrysum italicum
Heuchera micrantha 'Palace Purple'
Heuchera 'Pewter Moon'
Iberis (most)
Lavandula angustifolia 'Munstead'
Potentilla alba
Veronica prostrata 'Trehane'
Viola 'Huntercombe Purple', *V.* 'Jackanapes'

PLANTS FOR CREVICES

Arenaria balearica, *A. montana*
Campanula cochleariifolia
Chamaemelum nobile 'Treneague'
Leptinella atrata
Mentha requienii
Sempervivum (most)
Soleirolia soleirolii
Thymus pseudolanuginosus, *T. serpyllum*

CONCRETES AND MORTARS

CONCRETE IS A FAR MORE VERSATILE surface than its drab image suggests. Apart from the fact that it is relatively quick and easy to lay, it can be painted and textured to create a totally new surface while retaining the qualities of durability and resilience. It is also an excellent matrix in which to set materials such as cobblestones and other decorative aggregates.

LAYING CONCRETE

A plain stretch of concrete (*see next page*) can be just what you need – for a driveway, perhaps – but you can also use concrete and mortar mixes as bases in which to create interesting textures. Use a stiff-bristled broom to add contrast by exposing aggregate (*p.44*), or inset pebbles (*p.45*), cobbles or glass nuggets to create mosaic effects. Alternatively, leaves, seashells and other natural forms make effective stamped patterns (*p.46*) in concrete.

WORKING WITH CEMENT

- If the site to be concreted is large, divide it into smaller sections no bigger than 4m long.
- If mixing your own concrete, start by adding one part water to two parts cement and then gradually add more water.
- If the mixture gets too wet, sprinkle in a small amount of dry cement and quickly work it in, making sure that no lumps form.
- Avoid laying concrete if the temperature is close to freezing or over 32°C.
- Store bags of cement on raised planks and cover with a plastic sheet to keep dry.

PEBBLE INLAY *Making a feature of mortar pointing between slabs, by studding it with pebbles, adds variety and makes expensive paving materials go further.*

◀ PATTERNED FINISH *Glazed ceramic balls set in concrete can produce a stylish surface.*

YOU NEED:

MATERIALS

- 8 × 2.5cm wooden shuttering planks
- 5cm nails
- Hardcore to cover base area to 10cm
- Concrete to cover hardcore to 10cm
- Plastic sheeting

TOOLS

- Pegs, string, wood
- Builder's square
- Spade
- Spirit level
- Hammer
- Club hammer
- Roller
- Wooden beam
- Builder's trowel
- Builder's float

For areas over 4 sq.m, hiring a concrete mixer is advisable; they are usually available by the day or half-day.

MAKING A WOODEN FRAMEWORK

1 **Having marked out** the site (*see p.26, step 1*), dig it out to a depth of 20cm and drive levelling pegs into the ground 1m apart along string lines. Align them horizontally using a plank of wood and a spirit level.

2 **Remove** the string lines and nail wooden planks to the inner faces of the pegs, butted end-to-end at the corners. Use a club hammer to hold the plank steady. This framework holds the concrete in place until it sets hard.

ADDING A HARDCORE BASE

3 **Spread hardcore** 10cm deep over the subsoil. If the area is large, use planks to divide into 4m sections, to allow for expansion joints, without which concrete may crack.

4 **Tamp the hardcore** down thoroughly with a roller or stout timber post to ensure that there are no voids or air pockets between the hardcore and subsoil base.

Laying the Concrete

5 Tip concrete into the first section – the depth should be 10cm – and spread level so it is just proud of the framework. Work well into the edges with a spade or builder's trowel.

6 Use a wooden beam, slightly longer than the width of the framework, to compact the concrete with a downward chopping motion. This will remove any air pockets.

7 Slide the beam from side to side to level any rises in the surface and fill any remaining hollows with fresh concrete. Level the surface one more time and finish off using a builder's float.

8 Place a protective, waterproof covering such as plastic sheeting over the concrete and leave for about 10 days. This will trap moisture and help cure the concrete. Remove the framework when the concrete has set hard.

PAINTING CONCRETE

Concrete takes one month to set fully, after which it can be painted with a number of different products. Patio sealant (*right*) does just that, adding an extra layer of protection to the concrete together with a coloured pigment. Staining is another method, though you should allow at least 6 weeks from laying fresh concrete before applying the stain. Semi-transparent wood stains take well on concrete. Special concrete paints offer the widest choice of colours, with water-based latex paint being the most effective. Apply 2 or 3 coats.

SEALING CONCRETE

Using Decorative Aggregates

Aggregates are usually incorporated to provide cohesion to a concrete mix, but if you choose an attractively coloured gravel, it can be exposed to create a decorative surface finish that offers an alternative to plain concrete (*see p.43*). Different grades can be used for specific finishes; fine-grade gravel, for example, gives a fine-textured surface that is comfortable to walk on. As for plain concrete, aggregates should be laid over a hardcore base (*see p.42*).

Exposed Aggregate

YOU NEED:

MATERIALS
- Concrete mix
- Pebbles (or other aggregates, depending on required finish)

TOOLS
- Spade
- Wooden beam
- Stiff-bristled brush

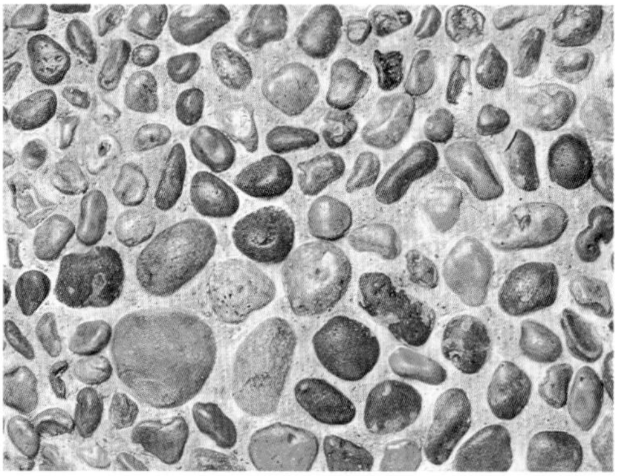

SELECTING A FINISH *Differing grades of gravel, pea shingle or pebbles give the surface a fine or coarse texture. The colours of local materials usually blend best.*

1 **Mix concrete** and pebbles thoroughly and, using a spade, lay it onto a firm sub-base (*see p.42*). Compact it with a wooden beam then screed it level with the beam, but do not finish with a builder's float.

2 **Let the surface** dry for about 6 hours. Remove a thin top layer of concrete by sweeping with a stiff-bristled brush and washing with a fine spray of water. Be sure to leave at least two-thirds of each pebble embedded.

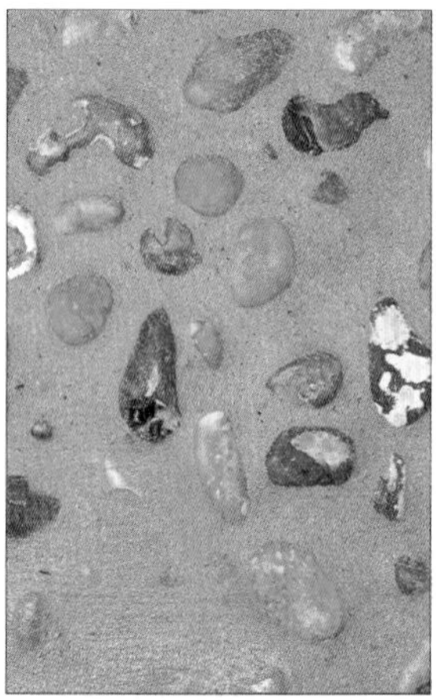

3 **Allow concrete** to cure for about 36–48 hours. When it is firm, clean any remaining cement residue from the aggregate with a high-pressure water jet or use a proprietary patio cleaner and rinse well.

Adding Textural Detail

If using pebbles or cobbles to add texture, bear in mind that such high-definition surfaces are difficult to walk on. This can be used to positive effect to deter walking on certain areas or, if purely decorative, can be confined to infills or the margins of an area. Pebbles and cobbles can be set by hand as a decorative surface layer into concrete or mortar. In either case, to ensure that they remain firmly fixed in place, they need to be embedded into the mix to a depth of at least two-thirds their height.

INFILLING SLABS WITH PEBBLES
Slabs fixed on bedding mortar make a secure surround. Set the pebbles into mortar by hand. Once in place, level them by pressing down firmly on a board laid across the slabs.

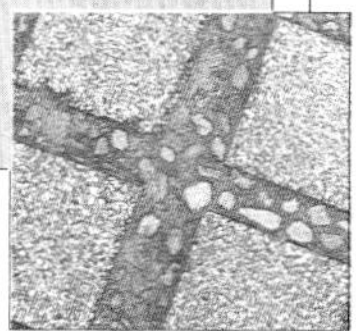

DECORATIVE MORTAR
Mortar studded with pebbles makes a decorative but secure restraint for widely spaced slabs. Remove the brick spacers before adding the mortar.

Laying a Pebble Mosaic

Decorative yet durable patterned surfaces can be created by setting pebbles into concrete. Having prepared the base (*see p.36*), lay the edges first. Visually divide the rest of the area into metre-square units and complete each one before moving on to the next. Don't attempt to lay the entire area at once – the concrete will have set hard before you finish.

MOSAIC WORK
When used imaginatively, restrained colours and simple materials can create a pleasing and detailed surface that is both durable and attractive.

STEPPING STONES

When cement is mixed, the setting process is a chemical reaction between limestone and water rather than a drying-out process. So concrete can be made in varying consistencies without significantly affecting its durability. If a fine aggregate like sand is used and it is mixed to a pouring consistency, it can be moulded into simple shapes to create stepping stones that are both stylish and hard-wearing. Apply imaginative decoration to add a highly individual element to your designs. A large, veined leaf has been used here, but a piece of tree bark, seashells or any other distinctive shape can be used.

MAKING STEPPING STONES

YOU NEED:

MATERIALS
- Board
- Plastic sheeting
- Plastic mould
- Oil for lubrication
- Large veined leaf
- Sand/cement mix (3 parts sand to 1 part cement)

TOOLS
- Straight-edge
- Mixing bucket

1 **Choose a mould** (here, cut from the top of a large flowerpot) about 5–7cm deep. Lubricate the inner surface with oil and lay it on a sheet of plastic on a flat, level surface or board. Place a leaf – veined surface uppermost – at the base. For best results, use a leaf with pronounced venation.

2 **To mix concrete,** add one part water to two parts of cement mix. Add concrete dye, if desired, then more water to achieve a pouring consistency. Fill mould to the brim.

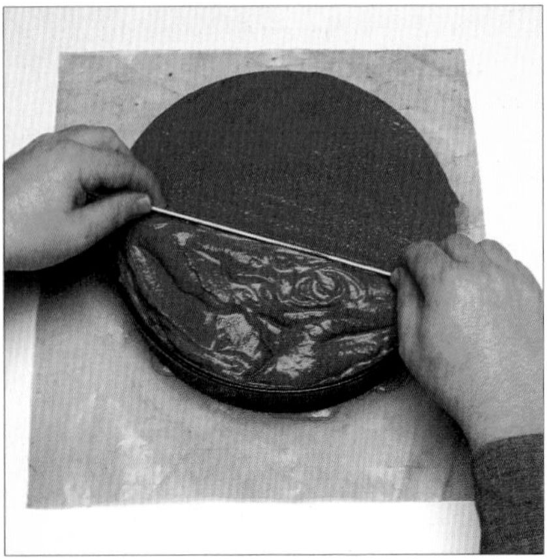

3 **Level off the excess** concrete using a straight-edge; drag it across the top of the mould to give an even and level surface. Put to one side to set.

4 When the concrete is firm, dry and fully set (about 3 days after pouring into the mould), lift the mould and its contents from the plastic sheet and invert it.

5 Apply a little pressure around the edge of the mould, pulling it outwards to ease stress on the stone when it is removed. Then slide the mould gently away from the stone.

6 Carefully pick away the leaf from the surface. Small remnants of leaf are best left to wear away naturally; don't try to scratch them off, you may damage the imprint.

7 The finished item is now ready to lay on sand and bedding mortar, as for ready-made slabs (*see p.27*). You can adapt the surface decoration to suit the location.

DECORATING CONCRETE

You can decorate concrete with almost any durable material, but you will find that rough-textured pieces will give the most secure bond. Arrange the material in the pattern of your choice on the surface of wet concrete, and push each piece in with a builder's float so that it lies just marginally below surface level. When the concrete is firm, sweep away excess concrete with a stiff-bristled brush and clean with a fine spray of water (*see p.44*). To remain securely fixed, inlays should be embedded to two-thirds of their depth.

FRAGMENTS OF TILE

OYSTER SHELLS

GLASS NUGGETS

BROKEN CROCKERY

Loose Surfaces

Loose materials, whether gravel, stone or bark chippings, are inexpensive, simple to lay and are the ideal choice for areas that incorporate curves – loose materials fill even the most awkward niches without complex cutting. Aesthetically, they create an intermediate texture between hard paving and the softer lines of planting and they provide an ecologically sound and labour-saving alternative to lawns, needing no feeding, watering or mowing.

A Simple Gravelled Area

If properly laid, gravel is a most versatile and practical medium. It makes a natural link between areas, plants can be planted through it for dramatic or subtle effect and it permits self-seeders to spread at the edges in pleasing drifts. But for ease of maintenance, for comfortable walking and free passage of wheelbarrows, it is most important to lay gravel on a firm, level and well-compacted sub-base, that is cleared of fertile topsoil and free of weeds.

CHOOSING GRAVEL

- Gravels are available in different grades and finishes, obtained as rough chippings from parent rock or as dredged, water-worn shingles. Choose a grade to suit your purpose. Grades less than 6mm create fine texture but are readily trodden into the house on the soles of shoes; any much larger than 12mm are uncomfortable to walk on.
- Obtaining gravels from a local source can save expense in transport and almost guarantees a colour range that blends effortlessly with the materials used in the house and other garden buildings.

ON THE EDGE *Loose gravel needs a restraining edge, especially where it meets soft surfaces like lawns. If kicked onto grass, it can be a potential hazard as it flies into the air when mown over. It may also damage the mower.*

◀ AREA OF TRANSITION *Gravel provides a unifying element between hard paving and soft plants.*

YOU NEED:

MATERIALS
- Equal parts small-grade finishing gravel and large-grade unprocessed gravel
- Bricks and mortar or planks and stakes to make holding edge

TOOLS
- Spade • Rake
- Wheelbarrow
- Plate compacter or heavy roller

PREPARING THE BASE

1 **Having chosen** your site, clear the ground of weeds (it is especially important to eradicate perennial weeds such as bindweed) and remove a 10cm layer of soil from the area. Edge the area with bricks in mortar or treated timber to keep gravel off the lawn. Alternatively, you can let it merge into a flower bed.

2 **To prepare** the base for gravelling, rake the soil level, then fill the excavated area with unprocessed gravel, or hoggin, almost back up to original ground level. Rake the surface completely flat.

3 **Using** a plate compacter (which can be hired) or heavy garden roller, compress the base to remove air pockets and thereby provide a stable base. The base needs to be compressed to at least 2cm below original ground level.

Laying the Gravel

4 Once you have achieved a firm, compacted base, add the finishing gravel, starting at one side and spreading it as you go.

5 Using a rake, work over the area to create an even surface. The finished level should be just below the edging so that gravel cannot stray onto the lawn. You may then decide to introduce some plants into the area, perhaps to soften edges near beds and borders or for architectural effect.

Planting in Gravel

1 Scrape the surface gravel to one side and dig a hole slightly larger than the plant's root ball through the gravel base and into the soil below.

2 Fill the hole with compost. Gently tease out the plant's roots, then plant so that it is almost level with the surrounding gravel.

3 Place some of the removed soil around the root ball and firm in. Replace gravel around the stem and under leaves, then water in.

Using Landscape Fabrics

The use of landscape fabrics, or geotextiles, makes laying gravel and other loose surface materials such as bark simple. Geotextiles, made from heat-bonded polypropylene, form a permeable barrier between soil and surface material, helping to suppress weeds yet allowing air and water to pass through. They are laid over the ground before planting and spreading the gravel or bark. The lightest weights are ideal in gardens and long-lasting.

Laying and Planting Through Geotextile

1 **Remove a layer** of soil 4–5cm deep, level the area and lay the geotextile over the surface. Secure the edges with small wire hoops to keep them flat. If gravel butts up to a lawn, install edging boards to keep the gravel in place.

2 **To plant through** the geotextile, make a cross-wise slit big enough to hold the root ball. Dig a planting hole and spread out plant roots. Backfill, firm in and water. Fold back the geotextile around the stem.

3 **Add the gravel** (or bark). Start at one side and spread it as you go, taking care not to damage plants. A 2–3cm layer gives sufficient coverage for most purposes. Finish by levelling with the back of rake.

How Geotextile Works

A geotextile fabric greatly extends the life of a gravel, bark or other loose surface, since it prevents chippings eventually becoming incorporated into the soil or sub-base. It makes a light-excluding layer that helps to prevent the germination of weed seeds. And because it is permeable to water and air, it does not deprive the soil and plant roots beneath of vital oxygen and moisture as black plastic sheeting does; neither does it allow the accumulation of surface water. Applications of fertilizer will be washed down to plant roots. Geotextile also offers the additional benefit of keeping plant roots cool in summer, and reduces their risk of freezing in winter.

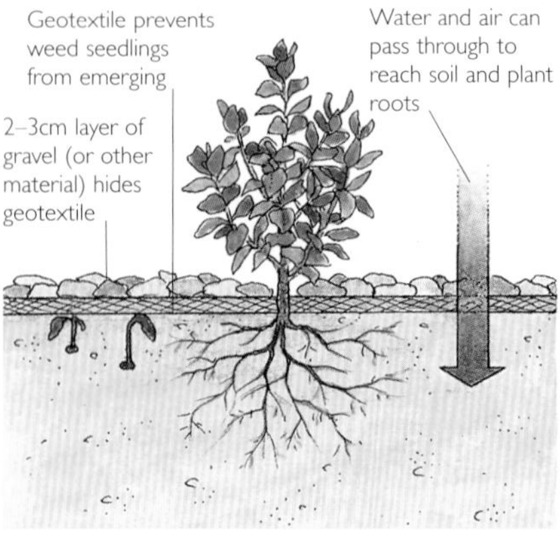

Plants for Gravel

Gravel drains freely and reflects light and heat so choose plants that enjoy these conditions. Drought-tolerant plants, such as silver-leaved plants from the Mediterranean, are ideal.

Rapid drainage also makes gravel an ideal home for robust alpines. Like plants that prefer dry conditions, these may succumb in winter wet. And gravel is a perfect foil for architectural plants.

IDEAL PLANTS
Plants with silvery leaves, like this group of verbascums, thrive in gravel; their foliage, especially if felted or hairy, is seen at its best – unsullied by soil and rain splash. The outlines of spiky architectural plants, like those of many grasses and phormiums, stand out beautifully. Self-seeding plants such as fennel (Foeniculum) *lend informality; be ruthless about pulling out unwanted seedlings or cut off heads before seeds can disperse.*

GOOD CHOICES FOR GRAVEL

FOR INFORMAL PLANTINGS

Anthemis tinctoria
Centranthus ruber (valerian)
Dictamnus albus
Dryas octopetala, D. drummondii
Foeniculum vulgare 'Purpureum' (bronze-leaved fennel)
Hyssopus officinalis (hyssop)
Lavandula (lavender), many
Lychnis coronaria
Origanum laevigatum
O. vulgare
Salvia officinalis (sage)

FOR ARCHITECTURAL IMPACT

Acanthus spinosus
Agapanthus 'Blue Giant'
Allium, many
Cynara cardunculus (cardoon)
Echium pininana
Eremurus robustus
Eryngium, many
Euphorbia characias and subsp. *wulfenii*
Phormium, many
Verbascum bombyciferum, *V.* 'Cotswold Queen', *V. olympicum*
Yucca flaccida, Y. gloriosa

PATHS THROUGH LOOSE MATERIALS

Areas of gravel or bark chippings often benefit from the inclusion of a pathway of firmer, sturdier materials. Stepping stones of timber, concrete (*see p.46*) or stone, or more heavyweight railway sleepers (*see facing page*), look decorative and prevent materials from being scattered or trampled down. In damp, shady woodland, a path like this will reduce the rate at which wood or bark chippings are naturally incorporated into the soil beneath.

STEPPING STONES

A gently curving line of stepping stones not only provides an irresistible invitation to explore a path, it also gives the opportunity to create patterns that are an integral part of the garden design. When incorporating stepping stones in a loose surface, the most pleasing results are to be had by selecting materials of a similar nature. Log sections or natural stone are the ideal choice for a woodland floor of bark chips or an area of gravel. Larger units such as railway sleepers are ideal for routes that take a lot of traffic, for instance a path that links two separate but frequently used areas of the garden.

MAKING THE PATH SAFE

- Lay small units on a firm sub-base and bed them on mortar to keep them secure and prevent gravel from working its way underneath and lifting the stepping stone.
- Keep the surface of stepping stones or sleepers as level as possible with the surrounding loose materials, to avoid tripping.
- Treat wooden materials with preservative before laying.
- Make sure that stepping stones have a non-slip surface; wood surfaces can be made safe by applying netting (*see p.69*).

OBVIOUS ROUTE
Light-coloured stepping stones show up well against bark chippings, reducing the risk of stumbling against the edges of the stones.

TEXTURAL HARMONY
Cross-sections from the trunk of a tree make a harmonious path across a floor of dried leaves in a shady woodland area.

Laying a Path of Railway Sleepers

1 **Dig out foundations** to create a firm, level base. The foundation trench needs to be slightly deeper than the height of the sleepers, to allow for a base layer of sharp sand.

2 **Bed the sleepers** on the sand in the desired pattern. Consolidate so that they are level and flush with surrounding surfaces. Lift carefully so as not to damage your back.

3 **When the sleepers** are in position, fill in the gaps with excavated soil. Consolidate by firming well with your heels. In dry weather, water the soil to aid compaction.

4 **Top off with gravel** to cover compacted earth. Use a heavy roller to consolidate it between the sleepers; make sure the finished surface is even and level with the sleepers.

5 **The finished** surface is not only practical, durable and easily negotiable, it blends perfectly with its surroundings. Sleepers are ideal for making a wide but curving path; the repetition of strong horizontal lines defines the course and leads the eye onward.

TIMBER DECKING

WOOD IS ONE OF THE WARMEST and most natural of materials to include in a garden. Though long used in building, when used for decking it is one of the most modern elements in garden design. Infinitely versatile, you can let its warmth shine through, or stain or paint it to suit your taste. And it is equally at home in situations as diverse as coastal gardens, smart urban courtyards and in wilder, more naturalistic, rural schemes.

MAKING A SIMPLE DECKING PLATFORM

Constructing an area of decking, like the platform below and overleaf, requires little in the way of building skills and no carpentry skills at all. Concrete walling blocks are used for the foundations, and laying the planks involves no woodwork joints. This construction method would suit a small patio or slightly raised boardwalk (*p.63*). Deeper, stouter joists would allow you to increase the height.

USING TIMBER OUTDOORS

- Use only timber that has been pressure-treated with preservative to extend its outdoor life. Most processes give the surface a greenish tinge. This will not affect the finished colour if you intend staining it, but if you want the warmth of natural wood, seek out special landscaping timbers that have been treated with colourless preservatives.
- Tropical hardwoods, such as iroko, combine great beauty with durability and, while very expensive, last a lifetime. But be sure that they come from sustainable forestry sources.

DESIGN AND CONSTRUCTION
This 2.5m square platform uses a building method (see next page) *that makes it easy to adjust size and shape. Tiny gaps between the planks allow the wood to swell when wet.*

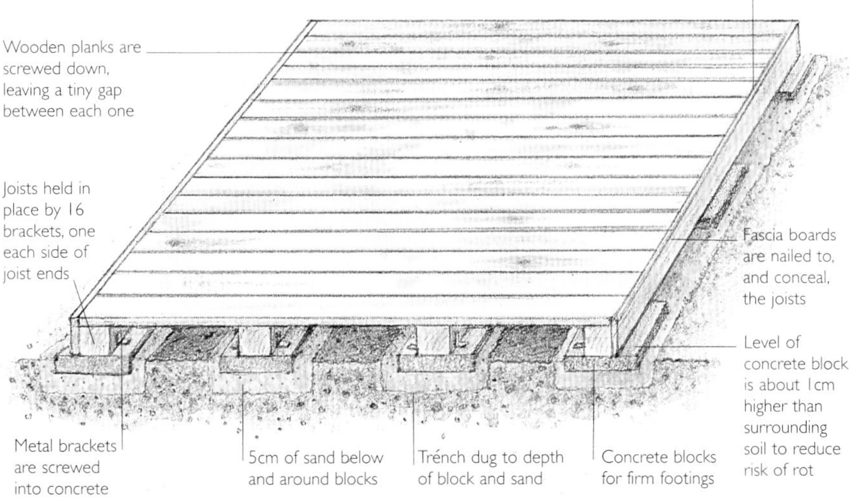

STAGGERED DECKING *Timber platforms float through an established planting.*

YOU NEED:

MATERIALS
- 16 planks 2.5m×15cm×2.5cm
- 4 wooden joists 2.5m×10cm×10cm
- 4 fascia boards, 2 measuring 2.5m×10cm×2cm and 2 2.54m×10cm×2cm
- 4 × 25kg bags sand
- 12 concrete walling blocks
- 16 metal 5cm angle brackets
- 5cm nails/screws
- Rawlplugs

TOOLS
- Spade • Spirit level
- Builder's square
- Club hammer
- Drill and drill bits

Planning the Site

1 **Measure out the decking area,** using 4 planks laid out in a square. Check that the corners form right angles by using a builder's square. The marked-out area will be 15cm larger than the desired 2.5m square platform, but the extra space will be needed for digging out the foundation trenches.

2 **Mark out** the boundaries of the work area by drawing the blade of a spade along the outside edges of the planks. Take care not to nudge the planks out of position before you have finished marking out the square. Put 3 of the planks to one side until later.

3 **Lay the joists,** parallel to each other within the square so that they are evenly spaced. Use one 2.5m plank to ensure that the first and last joists lie flush with the ends of the plank. Mark out a 15cm wide border around each joist to determine where the trenches should be.

Preparing the Base of the Decking

1 **Dig out the trenches.** They should be 4cm deeper than the depth of the precast concrete blocks. Line the base of each trench with sand, then firm it by treading it down and level it so that it forms a 5cm deep bed.

2 **Lay the concrete blocks**, 3 to a trench, placing one block at each end of a trench and one in the centre. The blocks should stand proud of the soil by 1cm so that the joists will not come into contact with the soil.

3 **Check the level** of the blocks, both along and across the trenches, using a plank and a spirit level. If necessary, adjust the level of any block: lift it and add a little more sand or gently knock it down with the handle of your hammer. Check the levels again.

4 **Backfill each trench** around the blocks with more sand, treading it down as you go to create a firm base. If not compacted, the sand bed will settle naturally, the blocks will shift or sink and the decking will warp. Level off the sand so that it is flush with the surface of the soil.

Constructing the Platform

1 Lay the joists across the concrete blocks and centre them on the blocks. Check again that the first and last joists are exactly 2.5m apart, using one of the planks. The ends of all the joists should also be in line.

2 Secure the joists in place using the metal brackets, one either side of each end of the joists. Place each bracket in position and mark the screw holes, one on the joist and one on the supporting block. Remove the bracket.

3 Drill the screw holes to a depth of 5cm, using a suitably-sized masonry bit for the concrete and a wooden drill bit for the joist. Insert rawlplugs into the concrete. Screw the bracket in place. Each joist requires 4 brackets.

4 Fix the first plank into place. Lay it across all 4 joists so that its edge sits flush with the ends of the joists. Drill 2 screw holes per joist, drilling through the plank and about 5mm into the joist below. Then screw the plank in place. For a flush finish, use a special bit and countersink the screws.

5 Position all the planks across the joists, leaving a tiny space of 5–7mm between each plank. The last plank should sit flush with the ends of the joists. Check that the planks are evenly spaced, then screw into place as for the first plank (*see step 4*). The gaps between the planks allow the timbers to swell when wet without warping.

6 Fit the fascia boards, nailing them into place along the edges of the joists. Each board needs at least 4 nails to hold it. Secure 2 × 2.5m fascia boards across the ends of the joists, then fit 2 × 2.54m boards along the length of the joists, so that they overlap the first 2 boards neatly at each corner. Trim the corners, if needed.

RAISING DECKING LEVELS

Laying decking at different levels is one of the simplest ways of introducing a visually interesting change of height to an otherwise level garden. The simplest construction technique is to screw or bolt a second tier onto the first. If using the above method, run the second set of joists at right-angles to those used for the first tier, to give extra strength. The technique of altering the direction of the parallel slats lends an extra dimension of interest; it can also be used to emphasize and warn of a change in level. Diagonal slats are particularly effective.

NEW HEIGHTS
A second layer of decking gives an elevated view over the garden. When the slats are laid diagonally, they give a sense of movement.

Finishing the Timber

Since the range of wood finishes is now so extensive, check with your supplier that the one you have chosen suits the job in hand. Pressure-treated timber needs only occasional treatment with preservative but you may still wish to apply colour for decoration or to offset the dulling effects of weather.

Adding Colour

There are two basic ways of colouring wood: with paint or with stain. Exterior wood paints are opaque, with a "microporous" finish that allows timber to breathe and helps prevent peeling or cracking. Wood stains are translucent and darken and/or colour wood. They penetrate the surface, allowing the grain to show through. Exterior formulas often include preservative. All surfaces must be clean, dry and dust-free before treating. Before painting, wood will need priming and undercoating. Apply paint or stain with a good-quality brush in the direction of the grain.

NATURAL SHADES
Preservatives combined with stain are available in a good range of natural wood colours.

TEMPTING COLOURS
Wood dyes in a water, oil or solvent base provide a wide choice of colours. Oil-based ones are the easiest to apply as they dry slowly. If water-based, colour intensity can be enhanced by the addition of pigments.

Using Tiled Panels for Texture

Ready-made panels, some of which have a non-slip finish, come in a range of patterns perfect for introducing changes of texture. Use a chequerboard design, for instance, or create your own, larger and bolder version from panels of parallel slats. When laying ready-made panels, take accurate measurements and space the joists carefully so that the panels are securely supported.

FIXING IN PLACE
Brass screws and fittings are best, followed closely by galvanized. Since they do not rust, they will not leak stains onto surrounding timber and can be removed if repairs are needed.

CHEQUERBOARD HERRINGBONE PARALLEL SLATS ANGLED PARALLEL-JOINTED

BOARDWALKS AND BRIDGES

Narrow decking platforms may be used as boardwalks and simple bridges. There is no need to lay foundations for a boardwalk; simply lay the constructed platforms on level ground and fix them in position by knocking in short fence posts at 1–1.2m intervals on either side. A bridge does need foundations; for safety reasons it must be at least 60cm wide and have a span of no more than 2.5m. Cut the joists and cross-planks to the required length and width before laying foundations.

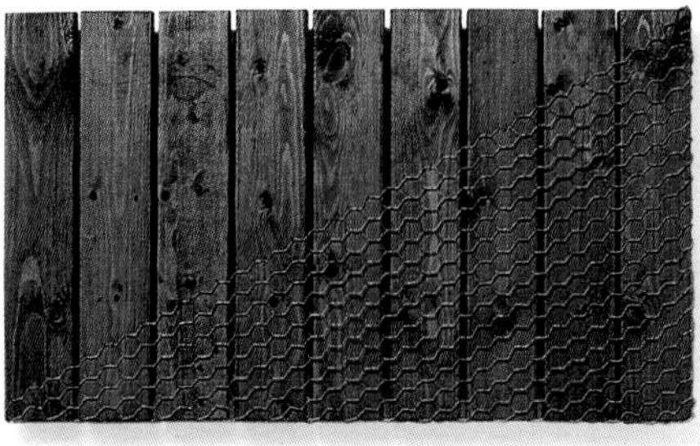

A NON-SLIP BOARDWALK
Timber becomes slippery when wet. Fine wire mesh nailed firmly over the boards makes an unobtrusive non-slip surface. Scrub the wood regularly to keep it free of moss and algae.

MAKING A BRIDGE

YOU NEED:

MATERIALS
- 8 pieces rough timber
- 2 × 50kg bags concrete
- 2 timber joists
- 4 × 12cm brackets and 8 × 5cm bolts and nuts
- Cross-planks
- 5cm, 8-gauge screws

TOOLS
- Spade, straight-edge, spirit level, screwdriver, drill

1 **Construct the foundations** for the bridge ends. Dig 2 holes 20–30cm wider than the bridge, 20cm across, 10cm deep. Use rough timbers and bricks to make rectangular forms. Fill in with concrete, using a straight-edge and spirit level to check both blocks are level with each other.

2 **Set the joists** across the blocks, at the required width apart and 10–15cm in from the edges. Mark where to put the bolts through the brackets. Embed the bolts in the concrete with 2.5cm of their screw ends exposed.

3 **Bolt on the brackets** when the concrete is dry. Remove the moulds and screw the joists to the brackets. Fix any liner under the bridge. Lay the cross-planks across the joists and secure in place as for decking (*see p.61*).

GETTING DOWN TO BASICS

CHOOSING MATERIALS

FOR MOST GARDENERS, the extensive choice of building materials available can be daunting – how do you select the right materials for the task in hand and how do you estimate quantities? In recent years, builders' merchants and DIY suppliers have made great efforts in the field of customer care and have become a good source of expert advice. But it helps enormously if you are familiar with the common materials and the terms used to describe them.

PAVING AND HARD SURFACES

Apart from cost, the intended use of a surface is a prime consideration. The greater the load, the stronger the sub-base and more durable the finish must be. For most garden surfaces, firm subsoil or a 10cm layer of hardcore topped with 5cm of sand is an adequate laying medium. Areas that must bear the weight of vehicles need a sub-base of 10cm of compacted hardcore with a further 10cm of concrete as a laying surface. Always seek expert advice before embarking on more ambitious projects.

PAVING UNITS

Paving slabs: cast or pressed concrete, reconstituted or real stone, in a range of colours and textures; 450×450mm, or 450×600mm are the most common sizes.

Clay pavers: small, durable units for bedding on sand, in a wide range of shapes, sizes and colours.

Bricks: wide range but of variable durability. Must be frost-proof and non-slip.

Setts: usually of granite, can last for centuries. Available as 75mm or 100mm cubes, or 225×100mm blocks.

Terracotta tiles: beautiful but porous and may crack if exposed to hard frost.

SURFACE FINISHES
Ensure that surface materials are totally weather-resistant, durable enough for the job in hand and provide a safe, non-slip walking surface when laid.

TERRACOTTA TILES

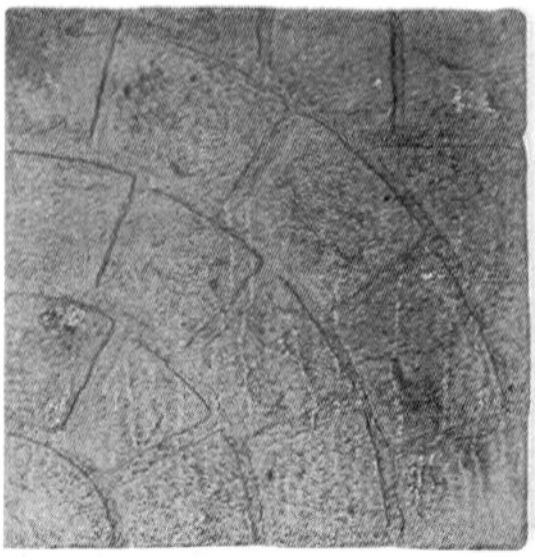

BRICK-PATTERNED PAVING SLAB

GRANITE SETTS

Loose Materials

Loose materials are used as decorative surface finishes and as aggregates in cement mixes; the grade (and cost) determines use. In general, the larger the grade and more decorative the appearance, the higher the cost. For decorative uses, size is important; it dictates how easily negotiable the surface will be. Use grit, pea shingle or small grade gravels for walking on; use cobbles for decoration and to restrict free passage.

COBBLES AND PEBBLES

GRAVEL

LOOSE MATERIALS

Aggregate: crushed stone or gravel used in making concrete; 20mm aggregate is suitable for most concreting jobs, larger grades are difficult to incorporate with hand tools.

Ballast: aggregate combined with sand, used in concrete mixes.

Hardcore: rubble, often made from broken bricks, used as a sub-base under concrete foundations.

Gravel: derived from chips of parent rock, e.g. limestone or Cotswold stone, or dredged, water-worn materials, e.g. fine grit and 6mm pea shingle. Comes in various grades; the smallest lend finer textures, and 12mm is about the maximum for walking comfort.

Cobbles and pebbles: rounded, water-worn stones of dredged or coastal extraction. Expensive, so used for decorative effects. Sizes range from 50–75mm to 175–250mm.

Concrete and Mortar

Concrete and mortar have different components and are used for different purposes (*see box, below right*). Bedding mortar is a mix of 1 part cement: 5 parts sharp sand. Masonry mortar is a mix of 1 part masonry cement: 3 parts soft sand.

For concrete for wall footings, foundations and bases for precast paving, mix 1 part cement, 2½ parts soft sand, to 3½ parts 20mm aggregate; for poured concrete: 1 part cement, 1½ parts sharp sand, to 2½ parts 20mm aggregate. All parts are by volume.

SOFT SAND

CEMENT POWDER

DRY MORTAR MIX

WET MORTAR MIX

USEFUL TERMS

Cement: a grey powder containing limestone. Mixed with water, it reacts to form the bonding agent in mortar and concrete.

Concrete: a mix of coarse aggregate, 5mm sand, cement and water that forms a hard-setting building or surface material.

Mortar: a mix of cement, sand and water for bonding bricks, stones or concrete slabs. Bedding mortar is used for laying and jointing paving; it is made with sharp sand rather than soft sand. Dry mix mortar is a stiff mix with less water used to fill paving joints. Masonry mortar, made with soft sand and masonry cement, is used for brickwork.

Sand: soft, or builders', sand is fine-grade and salt-free, and used for mortar mixes. Sharp sand is coarser; the 5mm grade used for concrete is sometimes called concreting sand.

Ordering and Quantities

When ordering materials, check transport and delivery arrangements and enquire about the supplier's "sale or return" policy; most reputable companies will accept returns of unused bagged materials if unopened. If you are using reclaimed materials from a salvage yard, however, you are more likely to be buying one-off parcels of material and their repeat availability may be limited. In this case, you need to make a careful estimate of your requirements to make sure that you have enough materials to complete the task.

CALCULATING QUANTITIES

Most reputable suppliers are happy to advise on the quantities of materials you will need to complete your job, provided that you tell them clearly the overall dimensions of the project in hand. To calculate volumes needed for regular areas simply multiply length by width by depth. For irregular areas, draw out the site on a piece of graph paper using a scale of one square to each square metre. Count all the complete squares and any that are more than one-third full. Multiply this figure by the depth to find the final volume.

ESTIMATING QUANTITIES
This 25kg bag of sand spread out to a 5cm layer yields a surprisingly small area, 75x75cm, in extent. It shows how difficult it can be for the inexperienced to calculate quantities, so don't be afraid to ask your supplier for expert advice.

Delivery and Storage

For most high-bulk building materials, suppliers will deliver straight to your door. If possible, try to arrange for delivery direct to the site to minimize the heavy labour of transporting them there later. You also need to give some forethought to storing the materials, since the volumes involved are likely to be considerable. If you intend to lay large areas of concrete, having ready-mixed concrete delivered makes the job a lot quicker and easier as long as there is easy access for large vehicles. The supplier will calculate volumes needed if given site dimensions and information about the intended use and load-bearings of the surface, but the site needs to be well-prepared in advance.

KEY CONSIDERATIONS

- By their very nature, building materials are often high volume, so consider carefully where they can be stored safely until you use them. Some items, like cement, need to be kept dry until used so will need a covered storage area or plastic sheeting.
- Shifting building materials is heavy work so try to recruit a team of helpers. This – and advanced preparation – is vital when taking delivery of ready-mixed concrete that must be dealt with quickly before it sets.
- In an ideal world, materials are delivered directly to the site, but if, for example, you live in a terrace, easy access may not be possible. If you need to carry materials through the house, take steps to protect interior walls and surfaces.

TOOLS FOR THE JOB

USING THE CORRECT TOOLS for the job always makes the task easier. Some simple items, such as a builder's square and float, can be made at home, while others, like a builder's screed (used for striking off to create a level surface) can effectively be substituted by a plank of wood. For smaller hardware, like builder's trowels, where quality and durability is less important than it is for professional use, the outlay need only be minimal; you can get away with the cheapest in the range.

INVESTING IN TOOLS

For some tasks, high-quality tools really make a difference to the finished article and this is especially true of measuring tools like tapes and levels. Accurate measurement is fundamental to a professional finish and it is well worth investing in the best you can afford. With proper care, they'll last a lifetime and you will undoubtedly find them useful for a variety of other projects. To ensure that tools perform and last well, they must be well-maintained. This is most important for tools used for concrete and mortar work, since these materials set hard if not cleaned off immediately after use. Metal parts and surfaces should be wiped over with an oily rag and stored in dry conditions to prevent rusting.

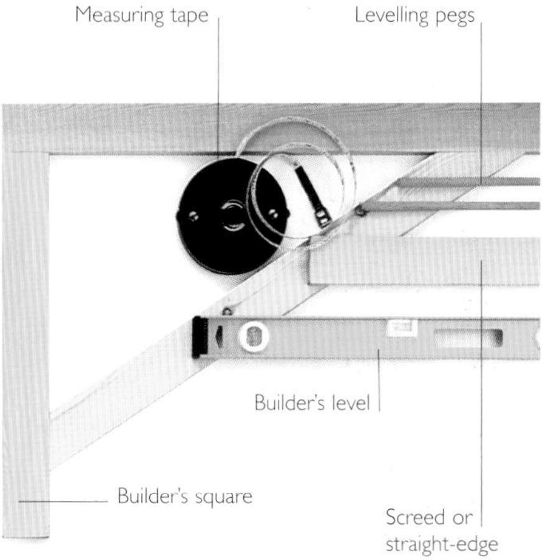

HIRING SPECIALIST EQUIPMENT

The heavy manual labour of mixing concrete and compacting sub-bases is only for the fit and strong, but specialist hire services carry a wide range of machinery to lighten the load. Some of the most useful items are stone or slab cutters, cement mixers and plate compacters. A good hire specialist can offer advice on the most suitable equipment for the job in hand and most hire by the full or half-day. It is most important, especially if you're unused to machinery, that you get a demonstration of how it works and how to use it safely; some of the best suppliers produce operating and safety literature. They may also supply any necessary protective gear, such as goggles and ear protectors.

PLATE COMPACTER
A mechanical compacter shortens the work of preparing sub-bases and laying flexible pavers, and is especially useful for large areas.

MAINTENANCE AND SAFETY

STATISTICALLY, GARDEN ACCIDENTS account for a significant proportion of home-based incidents and the potential for serious injury increases where you are using heavy machinery. Take all sensible precautions and check that all powered tools are in good repair. If you are unused to a tool or piece of machinery, ask advice when buying or hiring, or contact the manufacturer.

PROTECT YOURSELF

A stout pair of gloves is essential when dealing with mortar and concrete; the lime content can burn if it comes into contact with skin. Always use goggles to protect your eyes if dealing with loose materials and ear protectors when using equipment such as compacters and cement mixers. Wear close-fitting clothing when using any machine with moving parts and take special care to keep head, limbs and shovels clear when loading cement mixers. And even the professionals use kneelers or cushioned, waterproof knee pads, to make groundwork more comfortable.

GLOVES

KNEELERS

EAR PROTECTORS

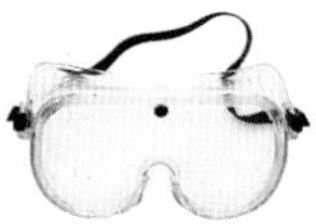
GOGGLES

LIFTING CORRECTLY
To protect your back, never lift by bending from the waist. Use the strength of your legs to lift the load, and carry heavy items close to the body. Don't overestimate your capabilities – remember that a load shared is a load halved.

INCORRECT LIFTING STANCE

CORRECT LIFTING STANCE

USING ELECTRICAL TOOLS

- The safe use of electrical tools depends on the observation of a few simple rules. One of the most important is the use of a residual current device (RCD), or earth leakage circuit breaker. If not already fitted, attach an RCD plug, or use an adaptor RCD between plug and socket.
- Do not use an electric tool during or just after rain as this may cause electrical faults.
- Always disconnect the power supply before adjusting, cleaning or inspecting a tool. And never touch a severed or damaged cable before disconnecting from the mains.
- Use leads that are only as long as necessary; trailing cables are potentially hazardous. Extension cables should have the same number of wires as the tool, and should be earthed.

Keeping Surfaces Safe

With the exception of gravelled areas, hard surfaces that are exposed to wet weather – especially in areas that are shaded or walked over infrequently – are likely to build up a slippery layer of algae, lichens or mosses. They can be removed with a stiff brush using a scrub of sharp sand and water, or treated with a proprietary patio cleaner. Wooden surfaces need regular maintenance. Once a year, check for splits and cracks and replace any damaged timbers. On wooden surfaces, fungal growths are inevitable in damp climates; they can be washed with a stiff brush and a mild solution of household bleach, or treated with proprietary fungicides. Small units, like wooden stepping stones, can be brushed clean with a wire brush. When using chemical cleaners, make sure that they are suitable for use with plants or take steps to protect them. This is especially important where surfaces are near to water; plant and animal pond life is extremely vulnerable to chemicals.

GETTING A GRIP
In damp or shaded areas, a covering of wire mesh will ensure a non-slip surface. Initially unattractive, it soon weathers into invisibility.

PREVENT SLIPPERY WOOD

- Nail fine-gauge chicken wire firmly in place onto wooden decking or stepping stones to provide an unobtrusive non-slip surface.
- Keep wood underfoot clean and free of algae by scouring regularly with a wire brush.
- If using chemical cleaning agents, make sure that they are safe to use near plants.

Controlling Weeds

You can control weeds on paving surfaces by hand-weeding, treating with a flame weeder, or using a chemical herbicide. Herbicides can be applied using a back-pack sprayer for large areas. On smaller areas, it is practical to use a dribble bar. Where ornamental plants are present, a spot-weeder is your weapon of choice.

WEEDS IN GRAVEL
Use a liquid herbicide to treat large areas. Reserve a clearly marked watering can with a dribble bar for dispensing liquid weedkillers.

ONE-TO-ONE ACTION
Spot-weeding is essential if weeds coexist with ornamentals. Use a weed wand or apply weed killer with a brush reserved for the purpose.

INDEX

Page numbers in ***italics*** indicate illustrations.

ACKNOWLEDGMENTS

Editorial contributors
Linden Hawthorne, Geoff Stebbings

Picture research Anna Grapes

Special photography Peter Anderson

Illustrations Karen Cochrane

Index Ella Skene

Dorling Kindersley would like to thank:
All staff at the RHS, in particular Susanne Mitchell, Barbara Haynes and Karen Wilson at Vincent Square; Annelise Evans, Candida Frith-Macdonald, Phil Hunt and Lesley Malkin for editorial assistance.

The Royal Horticultural Society
To learn more about the work of the Society, visit the RHS on the Internet at **www.rhs.org.uk**. Information includes news of events around the country, a horticultural database, international plant registers, results of plant trials and membership details.

Photography
The publisher would also like to thank the following for their kind permission to reproduce their photographs:
(key: t=top, c=centre, b=bottom, l=left, r=right, fj=front jacket, bj=back jacket)

DIY Photo Library: 67cr
Garden Picture Library: 9tl, 13tr; Brian Carter 9crb, 21crb, 28tl; Christi Carter 21tr; David Askham 22br; Gary Rogers 22tr, 40; Howard Rice 69tl; Jerry Pavia 8bl; Joanne Pavia 11t; John Glover 13tl, 14cr, 18br; Lamontagne 16br, 56; Philippe Bonduel 54bl; Ron Sutherland 14b, 16bl, 18cl, 20br, 22bl, 29tl, 30tr, 60tl; Tim MacMillan 34
John Glover: 32cr
Jerry Harpur: 10b, 41bl, 45bl
Clive Nichols: 19t, 48; design: Jean Bishop 7br, 12br, 15tl; Green Farm Plants/Piet Oudolf 53c; Save the Children – Chelsea 1991 28bl;
Elizabeth Whiting & Associates: 6; design: J King 24

Jacket: commissioned photography with the exception of **Garden Picture Library**: fj bl; Ron Sutherland fj cl, bj c; Jerry Pavia bj tl; John Glover bj tr; **Clive Nichols**: design Jean Bishop fj tl; **Steve Wooster**: fj l